John William Colenso

The Pentateuch and Book of Joshua

Critically Examined

John William Colenso

The Pentateuch and Book of Joshua
Critically Examined

ISBN/EAN: 9783742808486

Manufactured in Europe, USA, Canada, Australia, Japa

Cover: Foto ©Thomas Meinert / pixelio.de

Manufactured and distributed by brebook publishing software
(www.brebook.com)

John William Colenso

The Pentateuch and Book of Joshua

THE PENTATEUCH

AND BOOK OF JOSHUA

CRITICALLY EXAMINED

BY THE RIGHT REV.

JOHN WILLIAM COLENSO, D.D.

BISHOP OF NATAL.

'We can do nothing against the Truth, but for the Truth.'— *St. Paul*, 2 Cor. xiii. 8.

'Not to pretend, and not to fall short of, facts,—not to add, and not to take away,—to state the truth, the whole truth, and nothing but the truth,—are the great, the vital, maxims of Inductive Science, of English Law, and, let us add, of Christian Faith.'— *Quarterly Review* on 'Essays and Reviews,' Oct. 1861, p. 294.

SECOND EDITION, REVISED.

LONDON:
LONGMAN, GREEN, LONGMAN, ROBERTS, & GREEN.
1862.

PREFACE

THE SECOND EDITION.

———

THE demand for the First Edition of this book has been so rapid, that in the several impressions which have been called for I have not thought it necessary to distinguish different editions, although, from time to time, some verbal corrections have been made in the original text.

I have carefully studied all that has been said upon my book by writers of any kind, my sole object being to arrive at truth. These examinations, however, have not led me to doubt the accuracy of any of my conclusions. On the contrary, they have enabled me to establish, in this edition, still more decisively, some of my positions.

J. W. NATAL.

LONDON: 23 SUSSEX PLACE, W.
Nov. 21, 1862.

PREFACE.

The circumstances, under which this book has been written, will be best indicated by the following extracts from a letter, which I addressed some time ago, (though I did not forward it,) to a Professor of Divinity in one of our English Universities.

'My remembrance of the friendly intercourse, which I have enjoyed with you in former days, would be enough to assure me that you will excuse my troubling you on the present occasion, were I not also certain that, on far higher grounds, you will gladly lend what aid you can to a brother in distress, and in very great need of advice and assistance, such as few are better able to give than yourself. You will easily understand that, in this distant colony, I am far removed from the possibility of converse with those, who would be capable of appreciating my difficulties, and helping me with friendly sympathy and counsel. I have many friends in England; but there are few, to whom I would look more readily than to yourself, for the help which I need, from regard both to your public position and private character; and you have given evidence, moreover, in your published works, of that extensive reading and sound judg-

ment, the aid of which I specially require under my present
circumstances.

'You will, of course, expect that, since I have had the charge
of this Diocese, I have been closely occupied in the study of the
Zulu tongue, and in translating the Scriptures into it. Through
the blessing of God, I have now translated the New Testament
completely, and several parts of the Old, among the rest the
books of Genesis and Exodus. In this work I have been aided
by intelligent natives; and, having also published a Zulu
Grammar and Dictionary, I have acquired sufficient knowledge
of the language, to be able to have intimate communion with
the native mind, while thus engaged with them, so as not
only to avail myself freely of their criticisms, but to appreciate
fully their objections and difficulties. Thus, however, it has
happened that I have been brought again face to face with questions, which caused me some uneasiness in former days, but
with respect to which I was then enabled to satisfy my mind
sufficiently for practical purposes, and I had fondly hoped to
have laid the ghosts of them at last for ever. Engrossed with
parochial and other work in England, I did what, probably,
many other clergymen have done under similar circumstances,
— I contented myself with silencing, by means of the specious
explanations, which are given in most commentaries, the
ordinary objections against the historical character of the early
portions of the Old Testament, and settled down into a willing
acquiescence in the general truth of the narrative, whatever
difficulties might still hang about particular parts of it. In
short, the doctrinal and devotional portions of the Bible were
what were needed most in parochial duty. And, if a passage of
the Old Testament formed at any time the subject of a sermon,

it was easy to draw from it practical lessons of daily life, without examining closely into the historical truth of the narrative. It is true, there were one or two stories, which presented great difficulties, too prominent not to be noticed, and which were brought every now and then before us in the Lessons of the Church, such e.g. as the account of the Creation and the Deluge. But, on the whole, I found so much of Divine Light and Life in these and other parts of the Sacred Book, so much wherewith to feed my own soul and the souls of others, that I was content to take all this for granted, as being true in the main, however wonderful, and as being at least capable, in an extreme case, of *some* sufficient explanation.

'Here, however, as I have said, amidst my work in this land, I have been brought face to face with the very questions which I then put by. While translating the story of the Flood, I have had a simple-minded, but intelligent, native, — one with the docility of a child, but the reasoning powers of mature age, — look up, and ask, 'Is all that true? Do you really believe that all this happened thus, — that all the beasts, and birds, and creeping things, upon the earth, large and small, from hot countries and cold, came thus by pairs, and entered into the ark with Noah? And did Noah gather food for them *all*, for the beasts and birds of prey, as well as the rest?' My heart answered in the words of the Prophet, 'Shall a man speak lies in the Name of the Lord?' Zech. xiii.3. I dared not do so. My own knowledge of some branches of science, of Geology in particular, had been much increased since I left England; and I now knew for certain, on geological grounds, a fact, of which I had only had misgivings before, viz. that a *Universal* Deluge, such as the Bible manifestly speaks of, could not possibly have taken place in the way described in the Book of Genesis,·not to mention other difficulties which the story contains. I refer especially to the circumstance, well known to all geologists, (see LYELL's *Elementary Geology*, p.197,198,) that volcanic hills exist of immense extent in Auvergne and Languedoc, which must have been formed ages before the Noachian Deluge, and which are covered with light and loose substances, pumice-stone, &c., that must have been swept away by a Flood, but do not exhibit the slightest sign of having ever been so disturbed. Of course, I am well aware that some have attempted to show that Noah's Deluge was only a *partial* one. But such attempts have ever seemed to me to be made in the very teeth of the Scripture statements, which are as plain and explicit as words can possibly be. Nor is anything really gained by supposing the Deluge to have been partial. For, as waters must find their own level on the Earth's surface, without a special miracle, of which the Bible says nothing, a Flood, which should begin by covering the top of Ararat, (if that were conceivable,) or a much lower mountain, must necessarily become universal, and in due time sweep over the hills of Auvergne. Knowing this, I felt that I dared not, as a servant of the God of Truth, urge my brother man to believe that, which I did not myself believe, which I knew to be untrue, as a matter-of-fact, historical, narrative. I gave him, however, such a reply as satisfied him for the time, without throwing any discredit upon the general veracity of the Bible history.

' But I was thus driven, — against my will at first, I may truly say, — to search more deeply into these questions; and I have since done so, to the best of my power, with the means at my disposal in this colony. And now I tremble at the result of my

enquiries,—rather, I should do so, were it not that I believe
firmly in a God of Righteousness and Truth and Love, who both
'IS, and is a rewarder of them that diligently seek him.' Should
all else give way beneath me, I feel that His Everlasting Arms
are still under me. I am sure that the solid ground is there,
on which my feet can rest, in the knowledge of Him, 'in whom
I live, and move, and have my being,' who is my 'faithful
Creator,' my 'Almighty and most Merciful Father.' *That*
Truth I see with my spirit's eyes, once opened to the light of it,
as plainly as I see the Sun in the heavens. And that Truth,
I know, more or less distinctly apprehended, has been the food
of living men, the strength of brave souls that 'yearn for light,'
and battle for the right and the true, the support of struggling
and sorrow-stricken hearts, in all ages of the world, in all climes,
under all religions.'

[The letter then proceeded to state some of the principal
difficulties in the account of the Exodus, which are set forth at
full length in this volume, and concluded as follows.]

'Will you oblige me by telling me if you know of any books,
which to your own mind deal with these questions satisfactorily,
or, rather, will you kindly direct Messrs. —— to send to me the
book or books you may recommend, with others which I have
ordered from them? Among the rest, I have sent for HENG-
STENBERG's book on the Pentateuch, which I see commended in a
remarkable article in the Quarterly on 'Essays and Reviews.'
That article, however, appears to me to shrink from touching the
real question at issue, and, instead of meeting the essayists with
argument, to be chiefly occupied with pitying or censuring them.
Certainly, there are not a few points, on which I differ strongly
from those writers. But I cannot think it to be a fair way of

proceeding to point out, as the *apparent consequence* of the
course they are pursuing, that it will necessarily lead to infidelity
or atheism. It may be so with some; must it, therefore, be so
with all? The same, of course, might have been said, and probably was said, freely, and just as truly, by the Jews of St. Paul
and others, and, in later times, by members of the Romish
Church of our own Reformers. Our duty, surely, is to follow
the Truth, wherever it leads us, and to leave the consequences in
the hands of God. Moreover, in the only instance, where the
writer in the Quarterly does attempt to remove a difficulty, he
explains away a miracle by a piece of thorough ' neologianism,'
—I mean, where he accounts for the sun 'standing still,' at the
word of Joshua, by referring to ' one of the *thousand other
modes*, by which God's mighty power could have accomplished
that miracle, rather than by the actual suspension of the un-
broken career of the motion of the heavenly bodies in their ap-
pointed courses,' which last the Bible plainly speaks of to a
common understanding, though the writer seems not to believe
in it.*

---

* So, too, Archd. PRATT writes, *Scripture and Science not at variance*, p.25,—
'The accomplishment of this [miracle] is *supposed by some* [N.B.] to have been
by the arresting of the earth in its rotation. In what other words, then, could the
miracle have been expressed? Should it have been said, 'So the earth ceased to
revolve, and made the sun appear to stand still in the midst of heaven?' This is
not the language we should use, even in these days of scientific light. Were so
great a wonder again to appear, would even an astronomer, as he looked into the
heavens, exclaim, 'The earth stands still!'? Would he not be laughed at as a
pedant? Whereas, to use the language of appearances, and thus to imitate
the style of the Holy Scriptures themselves, would be most natural and intelligible.'
It will be observed that Archd. PRATT does not commit *himself* to maintaining the
above view: he says, 'it *is* supposed by some' to have been accomplished thus.
But he argues as if this explanation were possible, and not improbable; that is to
say, he lends the weight of his high position and mathematical celebrity to the

'After reading that article, I felt more hopelessly than ever
how hollow is the ground, upon which we have so long been
standing, with reference to the subject of the Inspiration of
Scripture. I see that there is a very general demand made
upon the clerical authors of 'Essays and Reviews,' that they
should leave the Church of England, or, at least, resign their
preferments. For my own part, however much I may dissent,
as I do, from some of their views, I am very far indeed from
judging them for remaining, as they still do, as ministers within
her pale,— knowing too well, by my own feelings, how dreadful
would be the wrench, to be torn from all one has loved and
revered, by going out of the Church. Perhaps, they may feel
it to be their duty to the Church itself, and to that which they
hold to be the Truth, to abide in their stations, unless they are
formally and legally excluded from them, and to claim for *all*

support of a view, which every natural philosopher will know to be wholly untenable. For,—not to speak of the fact, that, if the earth's motion were suddenly
stopped, a man's *feet* would be arrested, while his *body* was moving at the rate
(on the equator) of 1,000 miles an hour, (or, rather, 1,000 miles a *minute*, since
not only must the earth's diurnal rotation on its axis be stopped, but its annual
motion also through space), so that every human being and animal would be
dashed to pieces in a moment, and a mighty deluge overwhelm the earth,
unless all this were prevented by a profusion of miraculous interferences,—one
point is at once fatal to the above solution. Archd. Pratt quotes only the words,
'So the sun stood still in the midst of heaven, and hasted not to go down about a
whole day;' and, although this is surely one of the most prominent questions, in
respect of which it is asserted that 'Scripture and Science are at variance,' he dis-
misses the whole subject in a short note, and never even mentions the moon. But
the Bible says, '*The sun stood still, and the moon stayed*,' Jos. 13; and the arresting of the earth's motion, while it might cause the appearance of the sun 'standing
still,' would not account for the moon 'staying.'

It is impossible not to feel the force of Archd. Pratt's own observation, p. 30,
'The lesson we learn from this example is this: How possible it is that, even while
we are contending for truth, our minds may be enslaved to error by long-cherished
prepossessions!'

ber members, clerical as well as lay, that freedom of thought
and utterance, which is the very essence of our Protestant religion, and without which, indeed, in this age of advancing
science, the Church of England would soon become a mere dark
prison-house, in which the mind both of the teacher and the
taught would be fettered still with the chains of past ignorance,
instead of being, as we fondly believed, the very home of religious
liberty, and the centre of life and light for all the world. But,
whatever may be the fate of that book or its authors, it is
surely impossible to put down, in these days, the spirit of
honest, truth-seeking, investigation into such matters as these.
To attempt to do this, would only be like the futile endeavour
to sweep back the tide, which is rising at our very doors. This
is assuredly no time for such trifling. Instead of trying to do
this, or to throw up sandbanks, which may serve for the present
moment to hide from our view the swelling waters, it is plainly
our duty before God and Man to see that the foundations of our
faith are sound, and deeply laid in the very Truth itself.

'For myself, if I cannot find the means of doing away with
my present difficulties, I see not how I can retain my Episcopal
Office, in the discharge of which I must require from others a
solemn declaration, that they 'unfeignedly believe all the
Canonical Scriptures of the Old and New Testament,' which,
with the evidence now before me, it is impossible wholly to
believe in.*

'I need not say to you that, whatever support and comfort I
may feel in the consciousness of doing what appears to be right,
it would be no light thing for me, at my time of life, to be cast

* This was written before the recent decision of the Court of Arches, by which,
of course, the above conclusion is materially affected.

adrift upon the world, and have to begin life again under
heavy pressure and amidst all unfavourable circumstances,— to
be separated from many of my old friends, to have my name cast
out as evil even by some of them, and to have it trodden under
foot, as an unclean thing, by others, who do not know me,—not
to speak of the pain it would cause me to leave a work like this,
which has been committed to me in this land, to which my whole
heart and soul have been devoted, and for which, as it seemed,
God had fitted me in some measure more than for others,—a
work in which I would joyfully still, if it please God, spend and
be spent.

'But God's Will must be done. The Law of Truth must be
obeyed. I shall await your reply, before I take any course,
which may commit me in so serious a matter. And I feel that
I shall do right to take time for careful deliberation. Should
my difficulties not be removed, I shall, if God will, come to
England, and there again consult some of my friends. But then,
if the step must be taken, in God's Name I must take it; and He
Himself will provide for me future work on earth, of some kind
or other, if He has work for me to do.'

The above letter I wrote, but did not forward, in the early
part of 1861. I had not then gone so deeply into the question
as I have done since. And, as I do not wish to be misunderstood
by some, whom I truly esteem and love,— to whom I owe all
duty and respect, but allegiance to the Truth above all,—I may
here say that, at the time when I took counsel with my Episcopal Brethren at the Capetown Conference in January, 1861, I
had not even begun to enter on these enquiries, though I fully
intended to do so on my return to Natal. Then, however, I had

not the most distant idea of the results at which I have now
arrived. I am sensible, of course, that, in stating this, I lay
myself open to the objection, that the views, which I now hold,
are comparatively of recent date, and, having been adopted
within less than two years, may be found after a while untenable, and be as quickly abandoned. I do not myself see any
probability or possibility of this, so far as the *main* question is
concerned, viz. the unhistorical character of the story of the
Exodus, which is exhibited in the First Part of this work. But,
however this may be, I have thought it right to state the simple
truth. And, though these views are, comparatively speaking,
new to me,— and will be new, as I believe, to most of my
English readers, even to many of the Clergy, of whom, probably, few have examined the Pentateuch *closely* since they
took Orders, while parts of it some of them may never really
have *studied* at all,—yet I am by this time well aware that
most of the points here considered have been already brought
forward, though not exactly in the present form, by various
continental writers, with whom the critical and scientific study
of the Scriptures has made more progress than it has yet done
in England.*

Some, indeed, may be ready to say of this book, as the Quarterly
says of the Essayists, ‘the whole apparatus is *drawn bodily* from
the German Rationalists.’ This, however, is not the case; and

---

* HENGSTENBERG is very fond of representing almost all his opponents as *followers* of DE WETTE:—‘They supply themselves very freely from his stores, and
have made scarcely the least addition to them.’ Pent.ii.p.1. This, if true, would
tend to diminish the force of their multiplied testimony, and to reduce it to the
single voice of DE WETTE. But the same difficulties, *if they really exist, must,*
of course, occur to *all,* who bring a fair and searching criticism to bear upon the
subject, however they may differ in their mode of stating them.

I will, at once, state plainly to what extent I have been indebted
to German sources, in the original composition of this work.
Having determined that it was my duty, without loss of time, to
engage myself thoroughly in the task, of examining into the
foundations of the current belief in the historical credibility of
the Mosaic story, I wrote to a friend in England, and requested him
to send me some of the best books for entering on such a course
of study, begging him to forward to me books on both sides of
the question, 'both the bane and the antidote.' He sent me
two German works, EWALD (*Geschichte des Volkes Israel*, 7
vols.) and KURTZ (*History of the Old Covenant*, 3 vols.), the
former in German, the latter in an English translation (*Clark's
Theol. Libr.*), and a book, which maintains the ordinary view, of
the Mosaic origin and historical accuracy of the Pentateuch, with
great zeal and ability, as will be seen by the numerous extracts
which I have made from it in the body of this work. On receiving these books, I laid, for the present, EWALD on the shelf,
and devoted myself to the close study of KURTZ's work,—with
what result the contents of this volume will show. I then
grappled with EWALD's book, and studied it diligently, the parts
of it, at least, which concern the O.T. history. It certainly dis-
plays an immense amount of erudition, such as may well entitle
it to be called, as in the Ed. Review on 'Essays and Reviews,'
a 'noble work.' But, with respect to the Pentateuch, anyone,
who is well acquainted with it, will perceive that my conclusions,
on many important points, differ materially from his. Besides
these, I had, at first, two books of HENGSTENBERG, on the *Psalms*
and on the *Christology of the O.T.* And these comprised the
whole of my stock of German Theology, when the substance of
this book was written. Since then, however, and while rewriting

a

it with a view to publication, DR WETTE's *Einleitung*, and
BLEEK's excellent posthumous work, *Einleitung in das A.T.*,
have come into my hands. I have also carefully studied the most
able modern works, written in defence of the ordinary view, such
as HENGSTENBERG's *Dissertations on the Genuineness of the Pentateuch*, HÄVERNICK's *Introduction to the O.T.*, &c., with what
effect the contents of the present work will show. At a still
later period, I have been able to compare my results with those
of KEIL, in his *Historisch-Kritisch Onderzoek*, of which
Part I, on the Historical Books of the O.T., has just been
published at Leyden, (Sept. 1861,) — a work of rare merit, but
occupied wholly with critical and historical questions, such as
do not come into consideration at all in the First Part of the
present work. And, since my return to England, I have had an
opportunity of consulting Dr. DAVIDSON's *Introduction to the
O. T.*, Vols. I and II, the most able work which has yet appeared
in England on the subject of Biblical Criticism.

It will be observed that I have quoted repeatedly from
KURTZ, HENGSTENBERG, &c., as well as from English works of
eminence, written in support of the ordinary view. I have
made these quotations on principle, in order that the reader
may have before him all that, as far as I am aware, can be said
by the best writers on that side of the question, and may
perceive also that I have myself carefully considered the arguments of such writers, and have not hastily and lightly adopted
my present views; and I have often availed myself of their
language, in illustration of some point occurring in the course
of the enquiry, as being not only valuable on account of the
information given on good authority, but liable also to no
suspicion of having been composed from my own point of view,
for the purpose of maintaining my argument.

Being naturally unwilling in my present position, as a Bishop of the Church, to commit myself even to a friend on so grave a subject, if it could possibly be avoided, I determined to detain my letter when written, for a time, to see what effect further study and consideration would have upon my views. At the end of that time,—in a great measure, by my being made more fully aware of the utter helplessness of KURTZ and HENGSTENBERG, in their endeavours to meet the difficulties, which are raised by a closer study of the Pentateuch,—I became so convinced of the unhistorical* character of very considerable portions of the Mosaic narrative, that I decided not to forward my letter at all. I did not now need counsel or assistance to relieve my own personal doubts; in fact, I had no longer any doubts; my former misgivings had been changed to certainties. The matter was become much more serious. I saw that it concerned the whole Church,— not myself, and a few more only, whose minds might have been disturbed by making too much of minor difficulties and contra-

* I use the expression 'unhistorical' or 'not historically true' throughout, rather than 'fictitious,' since the word 'fiction' is frequently understood to imply a conscious dishonesty on the part of the writer, an intention to deceive. Yet, in writing the story of the Exodus, from the ancient legends of his people, the Scripture writer may have had no more consciousness of doing wrong or of practising historical deception, than Homer had, or any of the early Roman annalists. It is we, who do him wrong, and do wrong to the real excellence of the Scripture story, by maintaining that it must be historically true, and that the writer meant it to be received and believed as such, not only by his own countrymen, but by all mankind to the end of time. Besides which, it should be remembered always (as a friend has very justly observed) that, 'in forming an estimate of ancient documents, of the early Scriptures especially, we are doing that, which is like examining judicially the case of one who is absent, and unable to give his account of the matter. We should be very scrupulous about assuming that it is impossible to explain satisfactorily this or that apparent inconsistency, contradiction, or other anomaly, and charging him with dishonesty of purpose, considering that ours is an ex parte statement, and incapable of being submitted to the party against whom it is made.'

a 2

dictions, the force of which might be less felt by others. It was clear to me that difficulties, such as those which are set forth in the First Part of this book, would be felt, and realised in their full force, by most intelligent Englishmen, whether of the Clergy or Laity, who should once have had them clearly brought before their eyes, and have allowed their minds to rest upon them.* I considered, therefore, that I had not a right to ask of my friend privately beforehand a reply to my objections, with respect to which, as a Divinity Professor, he might, perhaps, ere long be required to express his opinion in his public capacity.

This conviction, which I have arrived at, of the *certainty* of the ground on which the *main* argument of my book rests, (viz.

---

* The following passage is written with a just appreciation of that 'love of positive, objective, truth,' which marks at least, if it does not specially distinguish, the English character. I cannot, however, give my assent to the closing words, which I have italicised, with the examples of Lycurgus, Numa, Zoroaster, &c., before me.

'One great characteristic of Englishmen,—the characteristic, in fact, on which they may justly rest their claims to a foremost (indeed *the* foremost) position among the representative races of humanity, is the belief in, and the love of, positive, objective, truth. . . . The Englishman may be narrow-minded or prejudiced, unapt to deal with abstract speculations. But he has, at least, had this training,— he has been accustomed to weigh evidence, *to seek for matter-of-fact truth in the first place*, and to satisfy himself as to the good faith and correct information of those, from whom he expects to receive knowledge or instruction. One thing with him is fixed and certain; whatever else is doubtful, this at least is sure: a narrative purporting to be one of positive facts, which is wholly or in any essential or considerable portion untrue, can *have no connection with the Divine, and cannot have any beneficial influence on mankind.*'—Rev. Preb. Cook, *Aids to Faith*, p.146.

To the same effect writes the Rev. H. J. Rose, *Replies to Essays and Reviews*, p.68:—

'We must never forget the difference between the German and the English mind. The paradise of the German appears to consist in unlimited license of speculation, while the *practical element* is the prevailing characteristic of the English. And thus it often happens that a German will not cast off a certain phase of faith, when he has demolished every ground, *which an Englishman would deem a rational and logical foundation for holding it.*'

To this strong, practical, love of truth in my fellow-countrymen, whether Clergy or Laity, I appeal in the present volume.

the proof that the account of the Exodus, whatever value it may
have, is *not historically true*,) must be my excuse to the reader
for the manner in which I have conducted the enquiry. A
friend, to whom I had submitted the work, before I had decided
to publish it, was afraid that I might give offence by stating too
plainly at the outset the end which I had in view. He thought
then — though now approving fully of the course which I am
taking—that such an open declaration of the sum and substance
of my work 'might tend to prejudice the reader, and probably
make him more inclined to become hardened against the force
of the arguments.' And he suggested that I might do more
wisely to conceal, as it were, my purpose for a time, and lead
the reader gradually on, till he 'would arrive of himself, almost
unawares,' at the same conclusions as my own. But, however
judicious for a merely rhetorical purpose such a course might
have been, I could not allow myself to adopt it here, in a matter
where such very important consequences are involved. I *must*
state the case plainly and fully from the first. I do not wish to
take the reader by surprise or to entrap him by guile. I wish
him to go forward with his eyes open, and to watch carefully
every step of the argument, with a full consciousness of the
momentous results to which it leads, and with a determination
to *test severely*, with all the power and skill he can bring to the
work, but yet to test *honestly* and *fairly*, the truth of every
inference which I have drawn, and every conclusion at which I
have arrived. As Dr. MOBERLY has well said, (*Some Remarks
on Essays and Reviews*) —

Those, who have the means of knowing, must not be content with a religion
on sufferance. The difficulties must be solved, and the objections must be met,
when they are produced in a serious and argumentative form. p.xxv.

A serious statement of difficulties is a thing to be highly respected and seriously replied to ; and, as to discussion, it would show great want of confidence in what we believe to be the truth of God, if we were afraid of allowing it, or of entering upon it, when gravely purposed and conducted. p.lxiii.

So, too, a plain and full statement of the case has been loudly called for by the most strenuous English defenders of the ordinary view of Scripture Inspiration. Thus the Rev. J. W. Burgon writes, *Inspiration and Interpretation*, p.xxxvi,—

We desiderate nothing so much as 'searching enquiry.' . . . If the writer would state a single case with its evidence, we should know how to deal with him. We should examine his arguments *seriatim*, and either refute them, or *admit their validity*. From such 'free handling' the cause of sacred Truth can never suffer.

And Prof. MANSEL writes, *Aids to Faith, p.12 :* —

Let us, at the outset, be clearly convinced of the vital importance of the question, in order that we may enter on its examination, prepared, if necessary, to sacrifice our most valued convictions at the demand of Truth, but, at the same time, so convinced of their value, as to be jealous of sacrificing them to anything but Truth.

I have, therefore, decided that it was my duty to give no 'uncertain sound,' but to set down openly at the outset the nature of the issue involved; and I trust that any plainness of speech in this respect will not be misinterpreted by my readers, as implying any wish or readiness on my part to utter what it may be painful to them, in their present state of mind, to hear. If my conclusions, indeed, were only *speculations*, if they were only matters of higher or lower *probability*, I feel that I should have no right to express them at all in this way, and thus, it may be, disturb painfully the faith of many. But the main result of my examination of the Pentateuch, — viz. that the narrative, whatever may be its value and meaning, cannot be regarded as historically true, — is not — unless I greatly deceive myself — a doubtful matter of speculation at all; it is a simple question of *facts*.

That the phenomena in the Pentateuch, to which I have
drawn attention in the first instance, and which show so decisively its unhistorical character, have not yet, as far as I am
aware, been set forth, in this form, before the eyes of English
readers, may, perhaps, be explained as follows:

(i) Some of these difficulties would only be likely to occur to
one in the same position as myself, engaged as a Missionary in
translating the Scriptures, and, therefore, compelled to discuss
all the minutest details with intelligent natives, whose mode of
life and habits, and even the nature of their country, so nearly
correspond to those of the ancient Israelites, that the very same
scenes are brought continually, as it were, before our eyes, and
vividly realised in a practical point of view, in a way in
which an English student would scarcely think of looking at them.

(ii) Such studies as these have made very little progress
as yet among the Clergy and Laity of *England*; and so the
English mind, with its practical common-sense, has scarcely yet
been brought to bear upon them. Add to which, that the study
of the Hebrew language has, till of late years, been very much
neglected in England in modern times.

(iii) The difficulties, which have been usually brought forward
in England, as affecting the historical character of the Pentateuch,
are those which concern the Creation, the Fall, and the Deluge;
and many, who feel these difficulties very strongly, are able to
get over them, by supposing the first two to embody some kind
of allegorical teaching, and the last to be a report of some
dread catastrophe, handed down in the form of a legend from
hoar antiquity, without questioning at all the general historical
truth of the story of the Exodus, upon which such important
consequences depend. Hence such minds are little impressed

by discussions mooted upon these points, and, indeed, are rather
irritated by having these questions brought before them at all,
when, as they think, they can be fairly disposed of.

(iv) Thus it is that English Books, upon the historical credibility of the Mosaic narrative, are at present very few, and still
fewer those, which treat the subject with the reverence due to a
question, which involves the dearest hopes, and fondest beliefs,
of so many; while others again, as the essays in ' Aids to Faith'
and ' Replies to Essays and Reviews,' which are written in
defence of the ordinary view, while professing a desire for
candid and free, though reverential, examination of the subject,
yet pass by entirely the main points of difficulty, as if they were
wholly unknown to the writers.

(v) It is not unlikely that the works of the (so-called) *orthodox*
German writers, HÄVERNICK, KURTZ, HENGSTENBERG, KEIL, &c.,
which are now being translated, and published in *Clark's Theological Library*, might before long have effected indirectly a considerable change in the current theology of England, by its being
seen how feebly they reply to some of the more striking objections,
which occur on a close study of the Pentateuch, — and which
many an English reader will often learn first from these very
attempts to answer them,—and also how often they are obliged,
by the force of the Truth itself, to abandon ground long held
sacred in England, of which several instances will appear in
the body of this book. But, even then, these portions of their
works are often so overlaid with a mass of German erudition, in
illustration of other questions of no consequence, about which
there is no doubt or dispute, that the reader is carried on from
one real difficulty to another, without being exactly satisfied on
each point as he passes, but yet without feeling very forcibly

the failure in each particular instance, his attention being
distracted, and his patience and perseverance often rather
painfully tasked, in the labour of going through the intermediate matter.

(vi) On the other hand, writers of the liberal school in
Germany take so completely for granted, — either on mere
critical grounds, or because they assume from the first the
utter impossibility of miracles or supernatural revelations, —
the unhistorical character and non-Mosaic origin of the greater
portion, at least, if not the whole, of the Pentateuch, that
they do not generally take the trouble to test the credibility
of the story, by entering into such matter-of-fact enquiries, as
are here made the basis of the whole argument.

There can be no doubt, however, that a very wide-spread
distrust does exist among the intelligent Laity in England, as
to the soundness of the ordinary view of Scripture Inspiration. But such distrust is generally grounded on one or two
objections, felt strongly, perhaps, but yet imperfectly apprehended, not on a devout and careful study of the whole question,
with deliberate consideration of all that can be said on both
sides of it. Hence it is rather secretly felt, than openly expressed; though it is sufficiently exhibited to the eye of a reflecting man in many outward signs of the times, and in none more
painfully than in the fact, which has been lamented by more
than one of the English Bench of Bishops, and which every
Colonial Bishop must still more sorrowfully confess, that the
great body of the more intelligent students of our Universities
no longer come forward to devote themselves to the service of
the Church, but are drafted off into other professions. How can

it be otherwise, when in an age like the present, — which has
been well described as one 'remarkable for fearlessness, and, it
may be hoped, for sincerity, in the pursuit of truth,' (Rev. Preb
Cook, *Aids to Faith*, p.133,) — the very condition of a young
man's entering the Ministry of the Church of England is, that
he surrender henceforth all freedom of thought, or, at least, of
utterance, upon the great questions which the age is rife in, and
solemnly bind himself for life to 'believe unfeignedly all the
Canonical Scriptures;' while he probably knows enough already
of geology, at all events, if not of the results of critical enquiry,
to feel that he cannot honestly profess to believe in them
implicitly? *   The Church of England must fall to the ground
by its own internal weakness, — by losing its hold upon the
growing intelligence of all classes, — unless some remedy be
very soon applied to this state of things. It is a miserable
policy, which now prevails, unworthy of the Truth itself, and one
which cannot long be maintained, to 'keep things quiet.'

Meanwhile, a restraint is put upon scientific enquiry of every
kind, by the fear of transgressing in some way the bounds,
which the Scripture statements are supposed to have set to such
speculations, and by the necessity of propitiating to some extent
the popular religious feeling on the subject.†   Men of science,

* This passage I have written, notwithstanding the relief given to the consciences
of many of the clergy by Dr. Lushington's recent judgment, because, if I mistake
not, the answer in the Ordination Service is not the only part of our formularies,
that will be generally understood, until explained by judicial authority, to involve
implicit belief in the historical truth of the facts recorded in the Pentateuch.

† A remarkable illustration of this may be seen in the fact that, even in such a
work as the English translation of Humboldt's *Cosmos*, 'undertaken in compliance
with the wish of Baron von Humboldt,' 'under the superintendence of Lieut. Col.
Edward Sabine, R.A., For. Sec. R.S.,' an important passage is omitted altogether, in which the expression of the author's views, as to the origin of the human

generally, have not the leisure to pursue very far for themselves
such investigations as these. And, if men of devout minds, they
will feel obliged to acquiesce, more or less, in the *dicta* of the
Church and the Clergy, while conscious oftentimes that such
dicta are painfully at variance with truths, which they have
begun to glimpse at as the results of their own researches.
They may proceed, and, probably, very many do proceed, far
enough to see that there is something hollow in the popular
belief, and that the modern view of Scripture Inspiration cannot
possibly be true in all points. But the work of examining into
its truth or falsehood is a work for theologians, not for natural
philosophers, and, to be done thoroughly, it requires great labour and a special training. Hence they will probably drop the
subject altogether, some sinking into practical, if even unavowed,
unbelief of the whole Mosaic story, as told in the Pentateuch,
others smothering up their misgivings with a general assumption
that the account must be substantially true; while there are
very many, who appreciate to some extent the difficulties of the
ordinary view, but yet are unable to satisfy themselves that it is
wholly untenable, and live in a state of painful uncertainty,
which they would gladly have terminated, though even by the

race from one pair, would have, perhaps, offended the religious prejudices of English readers. That the passage in question was not suppressed, by reason of any
change of view in HUMBOLDT himself, is shown by the fact that it is found in
the French translation, and the translator, M. FAYE, states as follows: 'Another
part, relative to the great question of human races, has been translated by M.
GUIGNAUT. This question was foreign to my habitual studies. Moreover, it has
been treated in the German work with such superiority of views and of style, that
M. de HUMBOLDT had to seek, among his friends, the man most capable of giving
its equivalent to French readers. M. de HUMBOLDT naturally addressed himself to
M. GUIGNAUT; and this savant has been pleased to undertake the translation of
the last ten pages of the text, as well as of the corresponding note.' (See *Indi-
genous Races of the Earth*, Trübner and Co., London, p.402–409.)

sharp pang of one decisive stroke, which shall sever their connection with it once and for ever.

I believe that there are not a few among the more highly
educated classes of society in England, and multitudes among
the more intelligent operatives, who are in danger of drifting
into irreligion and practical atheism, under this dim sense of
the unsoundness of the popular view, combined with a feeling
of distrust of their spiritual teachers, as if *these* must be either
ignorant of facts, which to themselves are patent, or, at least,
insensible to the difficulties which those facts involve, or else,
being aware of their existence, and feeling their importance, are
consciously ignoring them. It has been said by some, 'Why
make this disturbance? Why publish to the world matters
like these, about which theologians may have doubts?' I
answer, that they are not theologians only, who are troubled
with such doubts, and that we have a duty to discharge towards
that large body of our brethren,—*how* large it is impossible to
say, but, probably, much larger than is commonly imagined,—
who not only doubt, but disbelieve, many important parts of
the Mosaic narrative, as well as to those, whose faith may be
more simple and unenquiring, though not, therefore, necessarily,
more deep and sincere, than theirs. We cannot expect such as
these to look to us for comfort and help in their religious per-
plexities, if they cannot place entire confidence in our honesty
of purpose and good faith,—if they have any reason to suppose
that we are willing to keep back any part of the truth, and are
afraid to state the plain facts of the case.

On this subject I commend to the reader's attention the
following admirable remarks of Archbishop WHATELY, (*Bacon's
Essays*, with Annotations, p.11):—

We are bound never to countenance any erroneous opinion, however seemingly beneficial in its results, —never to connive at any salutary delusion (as it may appear), but to open the eyes (when opportunity offers, and in proportion as it offers) of those we are instructing, to any mistake they may labour under, though it may be one which leads them ultimately to a true result, and to one of which they might otherwise fail. The temptation to depart from this principle is sometimes excessively strong, because it will often be the case that men will be in some danger, in parting with a long-admitted error, of abandoning, at the same time, some truth they have been accustomed to connect with it. Accordingly, censures have been passed on the endeavours to enlighten the adherents of some erroneous churches, on the ground that many of them thence become atheists, and many, the wildest of fanatics. That this should have been in some instances the case, is highly probable; it is a natural result of the pernicious effects on the mind of any system of blind unenquiring acquiescence. Such a system is an evil spirit, which, we must expect, will cruelly rend and mangle the patient as it comes out of him, and will leave him half dead at its departure. There will often be, and oftener appear to be, danger in removing a mistake.—the danger that those, who have been long used to act rightly on erroneous principles, may fall of the desired conclusions when undeceived. In such cases, it requires a thorough love of truth, and a firm reliance on Divine support, to adhere steadily to the straight course. If we give way to a dread of danger from the inculcation of any truth, physical, moral, or religious, we manifest a want of faith in God's power, or in the will to maintain His own cause. There may be danger attendant on every truth, since there is none that may not be perverted by some, or that may not give offence to others; but, in the case of anything which plainly appears to be truth, every danger must be braved. We must maintain the truth as we have received it, and trust to Him, who is 'the Truth,' to prosper and defend it.

That we shall indeed best further His cause by fearless perseverance in an open and straight course, I am firmly persuaded. But it is not only when we perceive the mischiefs of falsehood and disguise, and the beneficial tendency of fairness and candour, that we are to be followers of truth. The trial of our faith is when we cannot perceive this; and the part of a lover of truth is, to follow her at all seeming hazards, after the example of Him, who 'came into the world, that He should bear witness to the Truth.'

For such persons especially, as I have indicated above, I have written this book, and for all, who would really see and know the actual Truth in this matter. I have desired to set before the reader at full length the arguments, by which I have been myself convinced upon the subject, and to take him with me, as it were, along the path, which I have followed in the search after the Truth. It is not sufficient merely to make general statements, or to refer to this or that writer, as having irrefragably proved the truth of certain results.* I have wished to enable the reader to satisfy his own mind on each point as it arises, precisely as I have satisfied mine, by a thorough discussion of all that can be said on both sides of the question.

Much labour has thus been bestowed, in the course of this work, in exposing the fallacy of very many of the arguments, which have been adduced by HENGSTENBERG and others, in support of the ordinary view. With reference to this point I sympathise entirely with the sentiments expressed in the following extract, quoted in *Types of Mankind*, Trübner and Co., *p.655*: —

> We should feel a humiliation to contend with such sophistries seriously and in detail, were we not firmly convinced that to do so is not merely the *most legitimate*, but also the *only*, mode, by which truth can be rendered permanently triumphant. Wit and sarcasm may obtain a temporary success; they may awaken minds otherwise prepared for freedom; but they are often unjust, usually unbenevolent, and consequently, in the majority of cases, they merely awaken antagonism, and cause men to cling with increased fondness to their opinions. Nothing but minute, search-

---

* This is a great defect in more than one of the Essays contained in the ‘Aids to Faith,’ arising chiefly, no doubt, from the very wide extent of ground which the whole controversy covers, and the limited space that could be allotted for each individual reply. But it is very unsatisfactory to be told, *p.248*, that ‘it has been shown by HÄVERNICK,’ or, *p.240*, that ‘HENGSTENBERG has established beyond all possibility of refutation’ some point under consideration, when (as will appear in numberless cases in the course of this work) an actual quotation and discussion of the arguments used in such cases would very probably show that they are anything but convincing or indisputable. So, too, the Essays, above referred to, deal for the most part with general questions, upon which it is easy to say much that is very true, and would be readily admitted, at least by one arguing from my point of view; whereas the *details* of the Scripture narrative, in which the real difficulties lie, are left by these writers for the most part unnoticed.

ing, inexorable, argument will ever obtain a speedy or a permanent triumph over deep-seated prejudices.

And, although by adopting this course, I have necessarily increased the size of my book, I could not do otherwise, if I would effectually compass the end which I have in view, and place the whole subject fairly and fully within the grasp of any earnest and intelligent enquirer, whether Clerk or Layman.

I have here confined my enquiries chiefly to the Pentateuch and book of Joshua, though, in so doing, I have found myself compelled to take more or less into consideration the other books of the Old Testament also. Should God in His Providence call me to the work, I shall not shrink from the duty of examining on behalf of others into the question, in what way the interpretation of the New Testament is affected by the unhistorical character of the Pentateuch. Of course, for the satisfaction of my own mind, and in the discharge of my duties to those more immediately dependent on me, I cannot avoid doing so, if health and strength are granted me, as soon as I have completed the present work, and ascertained that the ground is sure, on which I here take my stand. For the present, I have desired to follow the leading of the Truth itself, and not to distract my attention, or incur the temptation of falsifying the conclusions, to which the argument would honestly lead me, by taking account à priori of the consequences; and I would gladly leave to other hands the work of conducting the above enquiry at greater length for the general reader.

On one point, however, it may be well to make here a few observations. There may be some, who will say that such words as those in John vi.46,47, 'For had ye believed Moses, ye would have believed Me, for *he wrote* of Me. But, if ye believe not his writings, how shall ye believe my words?'—or in Luke xx.37, 'Now, that the dead are raised, even *Moses shewed at* the bush, [*i.e.* in the passage about the 'bush,'] when he called the LORD, the God of Abraham, and the God of Isaac, and the God of Jacob,'—or in Luke xvi.29, '*They have Moses* and the Prophets; let them hear them,' and *v.* 31, '*If they hear not Moses* and the Prophets, neither will they be persuaded, though one rose from the dead,'—are at once decisive upon the point of Moses' authorship of the Pentateuch, since they imply that our Lord Himself believed in it, and, consequently, to assert that Moses did *not* write these books, would be to contradict the words of Christ, and to impugn His veracity.

To make use of such an argument is, indeed, to bring the Sacred Ark itself into the battle-field, and to make belief in Christianity itself depend entirely upon the question whether Moses wrote the Pentateuch, or not. There is, however, no force in this particular objection, as will appear from the following considerations.

(i) First, such words as the above, if understood in their most literal sense, can only be supposed, at all events, to apply to *certain parts* of the Pentateuch; since most devout Christians will admit that the last chapter of Deuteronomy, which records the death of Moses, could not have been written by his hand, and the most orthodox commentators are obliged also to concede the probability of *some* other interpolations having been made in the original story. It would become, therefore, even thus, a question for a reverent criticism to determine what passages give signs of *not* having been written by Moses.

(ii) But, secondly, and more generally, it may be said that, in making use of such expressions, our Lord did but accommodate His words to the current popular language of the day, as when He speaks of God 'making His sun to rise,' Matt.v.45, or of the 'stars falling from heaven,' Matt.xxiv.29, or of Lazarus being 'carried by the angels into Abraham's bosom,' Luke xvi.22, or of the woman 'with a spirit of infirmity,' whom 'Satan had bound eighteen years,' Luke xiii.16, &c., without our being at all authorised in drawing from them scientific or psychological conclusions.

(iii) Lastly, it is perfectly consistent with the most entire and sincere belief in our Lord's Divinity, to hold, as many do, that, when He vouchsafed to become a 'Son of Man,' He took our nature fully, and voluntarily entered into all the conditions of humanity, and among others, into that which makes our growth in all ordinary knowledge *gradual* and *limited*. We are expressly told, in Luke ii.52, that 'Jesus increased in *wisdom*,' as well as in 'stature.' It is not supposed that, in His human nature, He was acquainted, more than any educated Jew of the age, with the mysteries of all modern sciences; nor, with St. Luke's expressions before us, can it be seriously maintained that, as an *infant* or *young child*, He possessed a knowledge, surpassing that of the most pious and learned adults of His nation, upon the subject of the authorship and age of the different portions of the Pentateuch. At what period, then, of His life upon earth, is it to be supposed that He had granted to Him, as the Son of Man, *supernaturally*, full and accurate information on these points, so that He should be expected to speak about the Pentateuch in other terms, than any other devout Jew of that day would have employed? Why should it be thought that He

b

would speak with certain *Divine* knowledge on this matter,
more than upon other matters of ordinary science or history?

While confining, however, as I have said, my present investigations to the Pentateuch and Book of Joshua, I have spared
no pains to make them as complete as possible, with the means at
my disposal, so far as these books are concerned. If it should bo
said that a work of this kind may well require years for its consideration, before it can be matured and fitted for publication,
I answer that, situated as I am, I have had no alternative.
Being invested with the episcopal office, I cannot, as an ordinary
clergyman might, obtain leave of absence from my duties for a
year or two, and have them carried on by a substitute. Nor
can I, arriving in England as a Missionary Bishop, and receiving,
therefore, calls from many quarters to plead the cause of Mis-
sions, decline acceding to such calls, without assigning, as I do
by the publication of this book, the reason why, with my present work in hand, I cannot comply with them. The question,
however, has been to me a matter of life and death, and I
have laboured upon it incessantly, with all the powers which
God has given me. Yet this toil has been mainly bestowed
upon the critical and subsidiary portion of my book; and, by a
careful comparison of my own conclusions with those of BLEEK
and KUENEN, which contain the latest results of continental criticism in Germany and Holland, I believe that I have made
myself sufficiently master of the subject, to be able to place confidence in the general soundness of the views that will be here
maintained, even though on some points, as will be seen, I feel
obliged to differ with the above eminent critics. The essential
portions, however, of this work, viz. the result arrived at in Part I,

required comparatively very little labour. The facts have only
to be stated, as I have endeavoured to state them, in a form
intelligible to the most unlearned layman; and the truth of the
conclusions drawn will, as it appears to me, be self-evident to
most of my readers, who have courage to face the truth, and
courage to confess it.

Finally, I am not aware of any breach of the Law of the
Church of England, as declared by the recent judgment in the
Court of Arches, which is involved in this publication. It is
now ruled that the words in the Ordination Service for Deacons,
'I do unfeignedly believe all the Canonical Scriptures,' must
be understood to mean simply the expression of a *bonâ fide*
belief, that 'the Holy Scriptures contain everything necessary
to salvation,' and 'to that extent they have the direct sanction
of the Almighty.'

I am not conscious of having said anything here, which con-
travenes this decision.   Should it be otherwise, and should the
strange phenomenon be witnessed, of a Bishop of the Protestant
Church of England, — more especially one, who has been expressly occupied in translating the Scriptures into a foreign
tongue, — being precluded by the Law of that Church from
entering upon a close, critical, examination of them, and from
bringing before the great body of the Church, (not the Clergy
only, but the Clergy and Laity,) the plain, honest, results of such
criticism, I must, of course, bear the consequences of my act.

But, meanwhile, I cannot but believe that our Church, representing, as it is supposed to do, the religious feeling of a free,
Protestant, nation, requires us now, as in the days of the Reformation, to protest against all perversion of the Truth, and all

suppression of it, for the sake of Peace, or by mere Authority. As a Bishop of that Church, I dissent entirely from the principle laid down by some, that such a question, as that which is here discussed, is not even an open question for an English clergyman,—that we are bound by solemn obligations to maintain certain views, on the points here involved, to our lives' end, or, at least, to *resign* our sacred office in the Church, as soon as ever we feel it impossible any longer to hold them.

On the contrary, I hold that the foundations of our National Church are laid upon the Truth itself, and not upon mere human prescriptions, and that the spirit of our Church, as declared in the days of the Reformation, fully recognises my right to use all the weight of that office, with which the Providence of God has invested me, in declaring the Truth, and recommending the subject of this work to the thoughtful consideration of English Churchmen. Nine years ago, I was deemed not unworthy to be called to this high office. I trust that the labours of those years may be accepted as an evidence that, to the best of my power, I have striven to discharge faithfully the duties entrusted to me, and may serve also as a guarantee, that, in putting forward this book, I am acting in no light spirit, but with the serious earnestness of one, who believes that he owes it as a duty to the Church itself, of which he is a minister, to do his part to secure for the Bible its due honour and authority, and save its devout readers from ascribing to it attributes of perfection and infallibility, which belong to God only, and which the Bible never claims for itself. More than all others, I believe, is a Bishop bound to do this, if his conscience impels him to it,—inasmuch as he, above others, is bound to be an example to the Flock of that walking in the Light, without

which there cannot be true Life in a Church, any more
than in an individual soul, — 'renouncing the hidden things
of dishonesty, not walking in craftiness nor handling the word
of God deceitfully, but, by manifestation of the Truth, commending himself to every man's conscience in the sight of God.'

If the arguments, on which the conclusions of these first
chapters rest, shall be found, upon a thorough examination, to
be substantially well-grounded and true, I trust that we shall
not rest until the system of our Church be reformed, and her
boundaries at the same time enlarged, to make her what a
National Church should be, the Mother of spiritual life to all
within the realm, embracing, as far as possible, all the piety,
and learning, and earnestness, and goodness, of the natio·.
Then, at last, would a stop be put to that internecine war
between the servants of one God and the professed followers of
the same religion, which now is a reproach to our Christian
name, and seriously impedes the progress of truth and charity,
both at home and abroad. Should the reception of this book,
by the more thoughtful portion of the community, indicate that
such a Reform is possible and probable, and will be but a
question of time, so that, being able meanwhile to speak out
plainly the truth, we shall have only to bear with the inconve-
niences and inconsistencies, which must attend a state of transition, it would not be necessary for me, or for those who think
with me, to leave the Church of England voluntarily, and
abandon the work to which we have devoted ourselves for life.

In conclusion, I commend this subject more especially to the
attention of the Laity. *They* are happy enough to be able to
lay aside such questions as these, if they will, while still con-
tinuing members of the National Church. I implore them to

---

consider the position, in which the *Clergy* will be placed, if the facts, brought forward in this book, are found to be substantially true. Let them examine their own hearts solemnly, in the sight of God, on these points. Would they have the Clergy bound, under pains and penalties, to profess belief in that, which they do not themselves believe in, to which they would not on any account commit themselves? Are they willing that their own sons, who may feel the Divine call to devote themselves to the ministry of souls, should be entangled in these trammels, so galling to the conscience, so injurious to their sense of truth and honesty, so impeding to the freedom and heartiness of their ministrations? *We*, indeed, who are already under the yoke, may have for a time to bear it, however painful it may be, while we struggle and hope on for deliverance. But what youth of noble mind, with a deep yearning for truth, and an ardent desire to tell out the love of God to man, will consent to put himself voluntarily into such fetters? It may be possible to represent some of the arguments in this book as invalid, others as unimportant. But, if the main result of it be true, as I believe it will be found to be, it seems to me impossible that, five years hence, unless liberty of speech on these matters be frankly acknowledged to belong to the Clergy as well as the Laity, any of the more hopeful and intelligent of our young men will be able, with clear consciences, to enter the ministry of the Church of England.

I now commit this First Part of my work into the Hands of Almighty God, beseeching Him mercifully to accept and bless it, as a feeble effort to advance the knowledge of His Truth in the world.

J. W. NATAL.

CONTENTS.

N.B. The quotations from Keith, Hengstenberg, and Havernick, are made from the English translations in *Clark's Theological Library*.

In a *double* quotation, such as E.viii.3 (vii.28) or D.v.20 (17), the second reference is to the Hebrew Text, which in such a case will be found to vary from the English Version.

PART I.

THE PENTATEUCH EXAMINED AS AN HISTORICAL NARRATIVE.

CHAPTER I.

1. THE first five books of the Bible,—commonly called the Pentateuch (ἡ πεντάτευχος βίβλος, Pentateuchus, sc. liber), or Book of Five Volumes,—are supposed by most English readers of the Bible to have been written by Moses, except the last chapter of Deuteronomy, which records the death of Moses, and which, of course, it is generally allowed, must have been added by another hand, perhaps that of Joshua. It is believed that Moses wrote under such special guidance and teaching of the Holy Spirit, that he was preserved from making any error in recording those matters, which came within his own cognisance, and was instructed also in respect of events, which took place before he was born,— before, indeed, there was a human being on the earth to take note of what was passing. He was in this way, it is supposed, enabled to write a true account of the Creation. And, though the accounts of the Fall and of the Flood, as well as of later events, which happened in the time of Abraham, Isaac, and Jacob, may have been handed down by tradition from one generation to another, and even, some of them, perhaps, written down in words, or represented In hieroglyphics, and Moses may, probably, have derived assistance from these sources also in the composition of his narrative, yet in all his statements, it is believed, he was under such constant control and superintendence of the Spirit of God, that he was kept from making any serious error, and certainly

B 2

from writing anything altogether untrue. We may rely with undoubting confidence — such is the statement usually made — on the historical veracity, and infallible accuracy, of the Mosaic narrative in all its main particulars. Thus, Archdeacon PRATT writes, *Science and Scripture not at variance, p.*102 : —

> By the inspiration of Holy Scripture I understand, that the Scriptures were written under the guidance of the Holy Spirit, who communicated to the writers facts before unknown, directed them in the selection of other facts already known, and *preserved them from error of every kind in the records they made.*

2. But, among the many results of that remarkable activity in scientific enquiry of every kind, which, by God's own gift, distinguishes the present age, this also must be reckoned, that attention and labour are now being bestowed, more closely and earnestly than ever before, to search into the real foundations for such a belief as this. As the Rev. A. W. HADDAN has well said, (*Replies to Essays and Reviews, p.*349,) —

> It is a time when religious questions are being sifted with an apparatus of knowledge, and with faculties and a temper of mind, seldom, if ever, before brought to bear upon them. The entire creation of new departments of knowledge, such as philology,—the discovery, as of things before absolutely unknown, of the physical history of the globe,—the rising from the grave, as it were, of whole periods of history contemporary with the Bible, through newly found or newly interpreted monuments, —the science of manuscripts and of settling texts,—all these, and many more that might be named, embrace in themselves a whole universe of knowledge bearing upon religion, and specially upon the Bible, to which our fathers were utter strangers. And beyond all these is the change in the very spirit of thought itself, equally great, and equally appropriate to the conditions of the present conflict,—the transformation of history by the critical weighing of evidence, by the separation from it of the subjective and the mythical, by the treatment of it in a living and real way,—*the advance in Biblical Criticism, which has undoubtedly arisen from the more thorough application to the Bible of the laws of human criticism.*

3. This must, in fact, be deemed, undoubtedly, *the* question of the present day, upon the reply to which depend vast and momentous interests. The time is come, as I believe, in the Providence of God, when this question can no longer be put by, — when it must be resolutely faced, and the whole matter fully and freely examined, if we would be faithful servants of the God

5

of Truth. Whatever the result may be, it is our bounden duty
to ' buy the truth ' at any cost, even at the sacrifice, if need be,
of much, which we have hitherto held to be most dear and precious. We are certain that He, who has given us our reasoning
powers, intends and requires us to use them, reverently and devoutly, but faithfully and diligently, in His service. We must
' try the spirits, whether they are of God '; we must ' prove all
things, and hold fast that which is good.' We must do this in
watchfulness and prayer, as those who desire only to know the
Will of God and do it. For, as Dr. DAVIDSON has truly said,
Introd. to the O.T. i.151,—

Piety, humility, and prayer are much needed here, by the side of acuteness and
learning.

4. For myself, I have become engaged in this enquiry, from
no wish or purpose of my own, but from the plain necessities of
my position as a Missionary Bishop. I feel, however, that I am
only drawn in with the stream, which in this our age is setting
steadily in this direction, and swelling visibly from day to day.
What the end may be, God only, the God of Truth, can foresee.
Meanwhile, believing and trusting in His guidance, I have
launched my bark upon the flood, and am carried along by
the waters. Most gladly would I have turned away from all
such investigations as these, if I *could* have done so,—as, in
fact, I did, until I could do so no longer. It is true that my
very office as a Clergyman, and much more as a Bishop, required me ' faithfully to exercise myself in the Holy Scriptures.'
But the study of the practical and devotional parts of Scripture
for a long time occupied me sufficiently, to satisfy my conscience in respect of this vow. And though, of course, aware—
as every thinking person must be—of some serious difficulties,
which present themselves in reading the earlier portions of the
Bible, I have been content to rest satisfied that the belief, in
which so many thousands of pious and able minds, of all ages
and countries, have acquiesced, must be,— in its main particulars, at least,— correct.

5. There was a time, indeed, in my life, before my attention
had been drawn to the facts, which make such a view impossible for most reflecting and enquiring minds, when I could
have heartily assented to such language as the following, which
BURGON, *Inspiration and Interpretation*, p.89, asserts to be the
creed of orthodox believers, and which, probably, expresses the
belief of many English Christians at the present day: —

> The BIBLE is none other than *the Voice of Him that sitteth upon the Throne!*
> Every book of it — every chapter of it — every verse of it — every word of it — every
> syllable of it — (where are we to stop?) every *letter* of it — is the direct utterance
> of the Most High! The Bible is none other than the Word of God — not some part
> of it more, some part of it less, but all alike, the utterance of Him who sitteth upon
> the Throne — absolute — faultless — unerring — supreme.

Such was the creed of the School in which I was educated.
God is my witness! what hours of wretchedness have I spent at
times, while reading the Bible devoutly from day to day, and
reverencing every word of it as the Word of God, when petty
contradictions met me, which seemed to my reason to conflict
with the notion of the absolute historical veracity of every part
of Scripture, and which, as I felt, *in the study of any other book*,
we should honestly treat as errors or misstatements, without in
the least detracting from the real value of the book! But, in
those days, I was taught that it was my duty to fling the suggestion from me at once, ' as if it were a loaded shell, shot into
the fortress of my soul,' or to stamp out desperately, as with an
iron heel, each spark of honest doubt, which God's own gift, the
love of Truth, had kindled in my bosom. And by many a
painful effort I succeeded in doing so for a season; though,
while thus dealing with my own doubts, I never certainly
presumed to think —with one who ' thanks God ' that ' the cold
shade of unbelief has never for an instant darkened his own
spirit ' — that each ' solitary doubter was paying the bitter
penalty, doubtless, of his sin (!),' BURGON, *p.ccix.*

6. I thank God that I was not able long to throw dust in the
eyes of my own mind, and do violence to the love of truth in

this way. With increase of mental power and general knowledge, it was, I felt, impossible to maintain the extreme view
above stated. And, without allowing that there actually were
any real contradictions, — without, in fact, caring to examine
too closely and curiously into the question, — yet, when feeling
the pressure of such difficulties, I have taken refuge, as I
imagine very many educated persons do in the present day, in
some such thoughts as those, which Prof. HAROLD BROWNE
recommends as a stay and support to the mind under such per-
plexities, *Aids to Faith*, p.317,318,—

If we believe that God has in different ages authorised certain persons to communicate objective truth to mankind, — if, in the Old Testament history and the
books of the Prophets, we find manifest indications of the Creator, — it is then a
secondary consideration, and a question in which we may safely agree to differ,
whether or not every book of the Old Testament was written so completely under
the dictation of God's Holy Spirit, that every word, not only doctrinal, but also
historical or *scientific*, must be infallibly correct and true. . . . Whatever conclusion may be arrived at, as to the infallibility of the writers on matters of *science* or of
history, still the whole collection of the books will be really the oracles of God, the
Scriptures of God, the record and depositary of God's supernatural revelations in
early times to men. . . . With all the pains and ingenuity, which have been
bestowed upon the subject, no charge of error, even in matters of human knowledge,
has ever yet been substantiated against any of the writers of Scripture. But, even
if it had been otherwise, is it not conceivable that there might have been infallible
Divine teaching in all things *spiritual* and *heavenly*, whilst, on mere matters of
history or of *daily life*, Prophets and Evangelists might have been suffered to write
as men? Even if this were true, we need not be perplexed or disquieted, so we
can be agreed that the divine element was ever such as to secure the infallible
truth of Scripture *in all things divine*.

7. But my labours, as a translator of the Bible, and a teacher
of intelligent catechumens, have brought me face to face with
questions, from which I had hitherto shrunk, but from which,
under the circumstances, I felt it would be a sinful abandonment
of duty any longer to turn away. I have, therefore, as in the
sight of God Most High, set myself deliberately to find the
answer to such questions, with, I trust and believe, a sincere
desire to know the Truth, as God wills us to know it, and with

a humble dependence on that Divine Teacher, who alone can guide us into that knowledge, and help us to use the light of our minds aright. The result of my enquiry is this, that I have arrived at the conviction, — as painful to myself at first, as it may be to my reader, though painful now no longer under the clear shining of the Light of Truth, — that the Pentateuch, as a whole, cannot possibly have been written by Moses, or by any one acquainted personally with the facts which it professes to describe, and, further, that the (so-called) Mosaic narrative, by whomsoever written, and though imparting to us, as I fully believe it does, revelations of the Divine Will and Character, cannot be regarded as *historically true*.

8. Let it be observed that I am not here speaking of a number of petty variations and contradictions, such as, on closer examination, are found to exist throughout the books, but which may be in many cases sufficiently explained, by alleging our ignorance of all the circumstances of the case, or by supposing some misplacement, or loss, or corruption, of the original manuscript, or by suggesting that a later writer has inserted his own gloss here and there, or even whole passages, which may contain facts or expressions at variance with the true Mosaic Books, and throwing an unmerited suspicion upon them. However perplexing such contradictions are, when found in a book which is believed to be divinely infallible, yet a humble and pious faith will gladly welcome the aid of a friendly criticism, to relieve it in this way of its doubts. I can truly say that I would do so heartily myself. Nor are the difficulties, to which I am now referring, of the same kind as those, which arise from considering the accounts of the Creation and the Deluge, (though these of themselves are very formidable,) or the stupendous character of certain miracles, as that of the sun and moon standing still, — or the waters of the river Jordan standing in heaps as solid walls, while the stream, we must suppose, was still running, — or the ass speaking with human voice, — or the miracles wrought by the magicians

of Egypt, such as the conversion of a rod into a snake, and the latter being endowed with life. They are not such, even, as are raised, when we regard the trivial nature of a vast number of conversations and commands, ascribed directly to Jehovah, especially the multiplied ceremonial minutiæ, laid down in the Levitical Law. They are not such, even, as must be started at once in most pious minds, when such words as these are read, professedly coming from the Holy and Blessed One, the Father and 'Faithful Creator' of all mankind :—

'If the master (of a Hebrew servant) have given him a wife, and she have borne him sons or daughters, *the wife and her children shall be her master's*, and he shall go out free by himself,' E.xxi.4 :

the wife and children in such a case being placed under the protection of such other words as these, —

'If a man smite his servant, or his maid, with a rod, and he die under his hand, he shall be surely punished. *Notwithstanding*, if he continue a day or two, he shall not be punished : for *he is his money.*' E.xxi.20,21.

9. I shall never forget the revulsion of feeling, with which a very intelligent Christian native, with whose help I was translating these words into the Zulu tongue, first heard them as words said to be uttered by the same great and gracious Being, whom I was teaching him to trust in and adore. His whole soul revolted against the notion, that the Great and Blessed God, the Merciful Father of all mankind, would speak of a servant or maid as mere 'money,' and allow a horrible crime to go unpunished, because the victim of the brutal usage had survived a few hours. My own heart and conscience at the time fully sympathised with his. But I then clung to the notion, that the main substance of the narrative was historically true. And I relieved his difficulty and my own for the present by telling him, that I supposed that such words as these were written down by Moses, and believed by him to have been divinely

given to him, because the thought of them arose in his heart,
as he conceived, by the inspiration of God, and that hence to all
such Laws he prefixed the formula, 'Jehovah said unto Moses,'
without it being on that account necessary for us to suppose that
they were actually spoken by the Almighty. This was, however,
a very great strain upon the cord, which bound me to the ordinary
belief in the historical veracity of the Pentateuch; and since
then that cord has snapped in twain altogether.

10. But I wish to repeat here most distinctly that my reason,
for no longer receiving the Pentateuch as historically true, is
not that I find insuperable difficulties with regard to the *miracles*,
or supernatural *revelations* of Almighty God, recorded in it,
but solely that I cannot, as a true man, consent any longer to
shut my eyes to the absolute, palpable, self-contradictions of
the narrative. The notion of miraculous or supernatural interferences does not present to my own mind the difficulties which
it seems to present to some. I could believe and receive the
miracles of Scripture heartily, if only they were authenticated
by a veracious history; though, if this is not the case with
the Pentateuch, any miracles, which rest on such an unstable
support, must necessarily fall to the ground with it. The language, therefore, of Prof. MANSEL, *Aids to Faith, p.9*, is wholly
inapplicable to the present case : —

The real question at issue, between the believer and the unbeliever in the Scripture miracles, is not whether they are established by sufficient testimony, but whether
they can be established by any testimony at all.

And I must equally demur to that of Prof. BROWNE, *Aids to
Faith*, *p.296*, who, in his Essay, admirable as it is for its general
candour and fairness, yet implies that doubts of the Divine
Authority of any portion of the Scriptures *must*, in all or most
cases, arise from 'unbelieving opinions,' while 'criticism comes
afterwards.' Of course, a *thorough searching* criticism *must*,
from the nature of the case, 'come afterwards.' But the 'unbelieving opinions' in my own case, and, I doubt not, in the

case of many others, have been the necessary consequence of my
having been led, in the plain course of my duty, to shake off
the Incubus of a dogmatic education, and steadily look one or
two facts in the face. In my case, critical enquiry to some
extent has preceded the formation of these opinions; but the
one has continually reacted on the other.

11. For the conviction of the unhistorical character of the
(so-called) Mosaic narrative seems to be forced upon us, by the
consideration of the many absolute *impossibilities* involved in
it, when treated as relating simple matters of fact, and without
taking account of any argument, which throws discredit on the
story merely by reason of the miracles, or supernatural appearances, recorded in it, or particular laws, speeches, and actions,
ascribed in it to the Divine Being. We need only consider
well the statements made in the books themselves, by whomsoever written, about matters which they profess to narrate as
facts of common history, — statements, which every Clergyman, at all events, and every Sunday-School Teacher, not to
say, every Christian, is surely bound to examine thoroughly,
and try to understand rightly, comparing one passage with
another, until he comprehends their actual meaning, and is
able to explain that meaning to others. If we do this, we
shall find them to contain a series of manifest contradictions
and inconsistencies, which leave us, it would seem, no alternative but to conclude that main portions of the story of the
Exodus, though based, probably, on some real historical foundation, yet are certainly not to be regarded as historically true.

12. The proofs, which seem to me to be conclusive on this
point, I feel it to be my duty, in the service of God and the Truth,
to lay before my fellow-men, not without a solemn sense of the
responsibility which I am thus incurring, and not without a
painful foreboding of the serious consequences which, in many
cases, may ensue from such a publication. There will be

some now, as in the time of the first preaching of Christianity, or in the days of the Reformation, who will seek to turn their liberty into a ' cloke of lasciviousness.' ' The unrighteous will be unrighteous still ; the filthy will be filthy still.' The heart, that is unclean and impure, will not fail to find excuse for indulging its lusts, from the notion that somehow the very principle of a living faith in GOD is shaken, because belief in the Pentateuch is shaken. But it is not so. Our belief in the Living GOD remains as sure as ever, though not the Pentateuch only, but the whole Bible, were removed. It is written on our hearts by GOD's own Finger, as surely as by the hand of the Apostle in the Bible, that ' GOD IS, and is a rewarder of them that diligently seek Him.' It is written there also, as plainly as in the Bible, that ' GOD is not mocked,'—that, ' whatsoever a man soweth, that shall he also reap,'—and that ' he that soweth to the flesh, shall of the flesh reap corruption.'

13. But there will be others of a different stamp,—meek, lowly, loving souls, who are walking daily with God, and have been taught to consider a belief in the historical veracity of the story of the Exodus an essential part of their religion, upon which, indeed, as it seems to them, the whole fabric of their faith and hope in God is based. It is not really so: the Light of God's Love did not shine less truly on pious minds, when Enoch ' walked with God' of old, though there was then no Bible in existence, than it does now. And it is, perhaps, God's Will that we shall be taught in this our day, among other precious lessons, not to build up our faith upon a Book, though it be the Bible itself, but to realise more truly the blessedness of knowing that He Himself, the Living God, our Father and Friend, is nearer and closer to us than any book can be,—that His Voice within the heart may be heard continually by the obedient child that listens for it, and that shall be our Teacher and Guide, in the path of duty, which is the path of life, when all other helpers —even the words of the Best of Books—may fail us.

14. In discharging, however, my present duty to God and to
the Church, I trust that I shall be preserved from saying a single
word that may cause *unnecessary* pain to those who now embrace
with all their hearts, as a primary article of Faith, the ordinary
view of Scripture Inspiration. *Pain*, I know, I must cause to
some. But I feel very deeply that it behoves every one, who
would write on such a subject as this, to remember how closely
the belief in the historical truth of every portion of the Bible
is interwoven, at the present time, in England, with the faith of
many, whose piety and charity may far surpass his own. He
must beware lest, even by rudeness or carelessness of speech, he
' offend one of these little ones ;' while yet he may feel it to be
his duty, as I do now, to tell out plainly the truth, as God, he
believes, has enabled him to see it. And that truth in the
present instance, as I have said, is this, that the Pentateuch,
as a whole, was not written by Moses, and that, with respect to
some, at least, of the chief portions of the story, it cannot be
regarded as historically true. It does not, on that account, cease
to ' contain the true Word of God,' to enjoin ' things necessary for
salvation,' to be ' profitable for doctrine, reproof, correction,
instruction in righteousness.' It still remains an integral portion of that Book, which, whatever intermixture it may show of
human elements, — of error, infirmity, passion, and ignorance,
— has yet, through God's Providence, and the special working
of His Spirit on the minds of its writers, been the means of
revealing to us His True Name, the Name of the only Living
and True God, and has all along been, and, as far as we know,
will never cease to be, the mightiest instrument in the hand of
the Divine Teacher, for awakening in our minds just conceptions
of His Character, and of His gracious and merciful dealings
with the children of men. Only we must not attempt to put
into the Bible what we think *ought* to be there: we must not
indulge that ' forward delusive faculty,' as Bishop BUTLER styles
the ' imagination,' and lay it down for certain beforehand that

God could only reveal Himself to us by means of an *infallible*
Book. We must be content to take the Bible as it is, and draw
from it those Lessons which it really contains. Accordingly, that
which I have done, or endeavoured to do, in this book, is to
make out from the Bible — at least, from the first part of it —
what account it gives of itself, what it really is, what, if we love
the truth, we must understand and believe it to be, what, if we
will speak the truth, we must represent it to be.

15. I shall omit for the present a number of plain, but less
obvious, indications of the main point which I have asserted;
because it may be possible, in some, at least, of such cases, to explain the meaning of the Scripture words in some way, so as to
make them agree with known facts, or with statements seemingly
contradictory, which are made elsewhere. My object will first be
to satisfy the reader's mind as soon as possible that the case is
certainly as I have stated it, that so he may go on with the less
hesitation, and pursue with me the much more difficult enquiry
into the real origin and meaning of these books. I shall endeavour to relieve him at once, in the very outset of our investigations, from that painful sense of fear and misgiving, which now,
I imagine, deters so many, as it has so long deterred me,
from looking resolutely and deliberately into the matter, and
applying to these books the same honest, though respectful, criticism, which they would apply to other writings, however highly
esteemed. So long as the spirit is oppressed with this sense of
dread, it is impossible to come to the consideration of the matter
before us with the calmness, and composure of mind, which the
case requires. In this way, also, we shall best be able to disen-
tangle the subject from the mass of sophistical arguments, which,
as will appear abundantly in the course of this work, have been
adduced by various writers in support of the ordinary view, and
which will never cease to be adduced by well-meaning writers,
and be eagerly acquiesced in by pious minds, so long as it is
assumed *à priori*, as an Article of Faith, that the Pentateuch, as

God's Word, is, therefore, also as an historical record, in all its parts, infallibly true, and that, consequently, *some* account *must* be given, however far-fetched and unsatisfactory, of the strange phenomena, which it presents to a thoughtful and enquiring reader.

16. It may not be easy, nor even possible, to determine with absolute certainty, when, and by whom, and under what peculiar circumstances, the different portions of the Pentateuch were written; though I shall hope to show, as we proceed, that much light may be thrown upon this point. But, in order to elucidate it more fully, we need the cooperation of many minds of different quality, who shall engage themselves vigorously in the enquiry, with the different talents which God has vouchsafed to them, and with the help of all the aids of modern science. At present there are but few, comparatively,— in England, at all events,— who have devoted themselves in a pious and reverent spirit to these studies. The number, indeed, of such students, is increasing, and will, I am sure, increase daily. But still there are not a few, who are unwilling to disturb, it may be, the repose of their souls, by examining into the fundamental truth of matters, which are believed, or, at least, acquiesced in, by the great mass of Christendom. And there are others, who dread lest, in making such enquiries, they shall, perhaps, be going 'beyond what is written,' and who shrink, as from an act of sacrilege, from the very thought of submitting, what they deem to be, in the most literal sense, the very Word of God, to human criticism.

17. Nevertheless, I believe, as I have said, that the time is come, in the ordering of God's Providence and in the history of the world, when such a work as this must be taken in hand, not in a light and scoffing spirit, but in that of a devout and living faith, which seeks only Truth, and follows fearlessly its footsteps, — when such questions as these must be asked, — be asked reverently, as by those who feel that they are treading

on holy ground,— but be asked firmly, as by those who would
be able to give an account of the hope which is in them, and to
know that the grounds are sure, on which they rest their trust
for time and for Eternity. The spirit, indeed, in which such
a work should be carried on, cannot be better described than
in the words of BURGON, who says, *p.*cxli :—

Approach the volume of Holy Scripture with the same candour, and in the same
unprejudiced spirit, with which you would approach any other famous book of high
antiquity. Study it with, at least, the same attention. Give, at least, equal heed
to *all* its statements. Acquaint yourself at least as industriously with its method
and principle, employing and applying either with at least equal fidelity in its
interpretation. *Above all, beware of playing tricks with its plain language.* Beware
of suppressing any part of the evidence which it supplies to its own meaning. Be
truthful, and unprejudiced, and honest, and consistent, and logical, and exact
throughout, in your work of interpretation.

And again he writes, commending a closer attention to Biblical
studies to the younger members of the University of Oxford,
*p.*12,—

I contemplate the continued exercise of a most curious and prying, as well as a
most vigilant and observing, eye. No difficulty is to be neglected; no peculiarity
of expression is to be disregarded; no minute detail is to be overlooked. The hint,
let fall in an earlier chapter, is to be compared with a hint let fall in the later place.
Do they tally or not? And what follows?

Bishop BUTLER also truly observes, *Analogy of Religion*,
Part II, chap.viii,§.1,—

The Scripture-history in general is to be admitted as an authentic genuine
history, till somewhat positive be alleged sufficient to invalidate it.

But he adds —

*General incredibility in the things related, or inconsistence in the general turn of
the history, would prove it to be of no authority.*

CHAPTER IL

18. I shall now proceed to show, by means of a number of prominent instances, that the books of the Pentateuch, in their own account of the story which they profess to relate, contain such remarkable contradictions, and involve such plain impossibilities, that they cannot be regarded as true narratives of actual, historical, matters of fact. Without stopping here to speak of the many difficulties, which (as will appear hereafter) exist in the earlier parts of the history, I shall go on at once to consider the account of the Exodus itself, beginning with the very first step of it, the descent into Egypt.

19. *And the sons of Judah, Er, and Onan, and Shelah, and Pharez, and Zarah; but Er and Onan died in the land of Canaan; and the sons of Phares were Hezron and Hamul.* G.xlvi.12.

It appears to me to be certain that the writer here means to say that Hezron and Hamul were *born in the land of Canaan*, and were among the seventy persons, (including Jacob himself, and Joseph, and his two sons,) who *came into Egypt* with Jacob.

He repeats the words again and again:—

'These are the names of the children of Israel, which came *into Egypt*,' v.8;

'All the souls, that came *with Jacob into Egypt*, which came out of his loins, besides Jacob's sons' wives, were threescore

c

and six,' v.26,—which they would not be without Hezron and
Hamul;

'And the sons of Joseph, which were born him in Egypt,
were two souls: all the souls of the house of Jacob, which *came
into Egypt*, were threescore and ten.' v.27.

So again we read,—

'These are the names of the children of Israel, which *came
into Egypt*; every man and his household *came with Jacob*.
And all the souls, that came out of the loins of Jacob, were
seventy souls; for Joseph was in Egypt already.' E.i.1,5.

'Thy fathers *went down into Egypt* with threescore and ten
persons; and now the LORD thy God hath made thee as the
stars of heaven for multitude.' D.x.22.

I assume, then, that it is absolutely undeniable that the
narrative of the Exodus distinctly involves the statement, that
the sixty-six persons, 'out of the loins of Jacob,' mentioned in
G.xlvi, and no others, went down with him into Egypt.

20. Now Judah was *forty-two* [*] years old, according to the
story, when he went down with Jacob into Egypt.

But, if we turn to G.xxxviii, we shall find that, in the course
of these forty-two years of Judah's life, the following events
are recorded to have happened.

(i) Judah grows up, marries a wife—'at that time,' v.1, that
is, after Joseph's being sold into Egypt, when he was 'seventeen
years old,' G.xxxvii. 2, and when Judah, consequently, was, at
least, *twenty* years old,—and has, separately, three sons by her.

(ii) The eldest of these three sons grows up, is married, and
dies.

---

[*] Joseph was thirty years old, when he 'stood before Pharaoh,' as governor of
the land of Egypt, G.xli.46; and from that time nine years elapsed, (seven of
plenty and two of famine,) before Jacob came down to Egypt. At that time,
therefore, Joseph was thirty-nine years old. But Judah was about three years
older than Joseph; for Judah was born in the *fourth* year of Jacob's double
marriage, G.xxix.35, and Joseph in the *seventh*, G.xxx.24-26, xxxi.41. Hence
Judah was forty-two years old when Jacob went down to Egypt.

The second grows to maturity, (suppose in another year,) marries his brother's widow, and dies.

The third grows to maturity, (suppose in another year still,) but declines to take his brother's widow to wife.

She then deceives Judah himself, conceives by him, and in due time bears him twins, Phares and Zarah.

(iii) One of these twins also grows to maturity, and has two sons, Hezron and Hamul, born to him, before Jacob goes down into Egypt.

The above being certainly incredible, we are obliged to conclude that one of the two accounts must be untrue. Yet the statement, that Hezron and Hamul were born in the land of Canaan, is vouched so positively by the many passages above quoted, which sum up the 'seventy souls,' that, to give up this point, is to give up an essential part of the whole story. But then this point cannot be maintained, however essential to the narrative, without supposing that the other series of events had taken place beforehand, which we have seen to be incredible.

21. Let us now see how this part of the Bible is treated by those interpreters, who wish to maintain the authenticity and historical character of the Pentateuch, and whether they adhere to the principles of honest and truthful exposition, so admirably laid down in the following extracts:—

There is no attaining a satisfactory view of the mutual relations of Science and Scripture, till men make up their minds to do violence to neither, and to deal faithfully with both. On the very threshold, therefore, of such discussions as the present, we are encountered by the necessity for a candid, truthful, and impartial exegesis of the sacred text. This can never be honoured by being put to the torture. We ought to harbour no hankering after so-called 'reconciliations,' or allow these to warp in the very least our rendering of the record. It is our business to decipher, not to prompt,— to keep our ears open to what the Scripture says, not to exercise our ingenuity on what it can be made to say. We must purge our minds at once of that order of prepossessions, which is incident to an over timid faith, and, not less scrupulously, of those counter-prejudices, which beset a jaundiced and captious scepticism. For there may be an eagerness to magnify, and even to invent, difficulties, as well as an anxiety to muffle them up, and smooth them over, — of which last, the least pleasing shape is an affectation of contempt, disguising obvious perplexity and trepidation. Those, who seek the repose of Truth, had best banish from the quest of it, in whatever field, the spirit and the methods of sophistry. *Replies to Essays and Reviews*, Rev. G. Rorison, p.277.

Let the interpreter then resolve, with God's assisting grace, to be candid and truthful. Let him fear not to state honestly the results of his own honest investigations; let him be simple, reverent, and plain-spoken; and, above all, let him pray against that sectarian bias, which, by importing its own foregone conclusions into the word of Scripture, and by refusing to see or to acknowledge what makes against its own prejudices, has proved the greatest known hindrance to all fair interpretation, and *has tended, more than anything else in the world, to check the free course of Divine Truth.* *Aids to Faith*, Dean Ellicott, p.421.

Those, however, who are satisfied that the above statements of the Bible do involve a manifest contradiction, and who are not interested in seeing how good men will 'do violence' to the plain meaning of the Scripture, in order to evade such a difficulty, may do well to omit the next Chapter altogether, and pass on to the arguments which follow.

CHAPTER III.

THE EXPLANATIONS OF EXPOSITORS CONSIDERED.

22. HÄVERNICK does not seem to be at all aware of the difficulty, and states the plain meaning of the passage as follows, *Pent. p.224*: —

We have now in G. xlvi the register of the tribes, introduced with genuine historical fidelity to truth. The comparison of it with the statements respecting the tribes in N.xxvi, and with the genealogies in Chronicles, puts its credibility (?) and its antiquity beyond doubt. For each of these genealogies rests upon the other: that which is contained in Genesis is expressly presupposed, and has been made use of in the two later ones. In connection with this, it is a circumstance not to be overlooked, that in Genesis we possess the *completest* list of Jacob's family. The deviations from it in the other genealogies are mainly confined to the omission of certain names. . . . This circumstance admits of a sufficient explanation only on the supposition that the sons, who were subsequently omitted, left no posterity behind them, on which account it would be intelligible that they should be passed over in the book of Numbers, where it is only families and races that are spoken of. *Our document is thus acquainted only with the original relations of Jacob's family, at the time that he went down into Egypt, and is quite unconcerned about its later formation.*

23. SCOTT writes:—

Judah was the fourth son of Leah, and Joseph was born when Jacob had been married about seven years. Consequently, Judah might be about three or four years older than Joseph; yet he could not be above forty-four at this time, for Joseph was only forty. His two sons, Er and Onan, had been married to Tamar, and a considerable time after their death had elapsed before Pharez was born. It can then hardly be conceived that this event took place much before Judah was forty years old. So that Pharez could not be more than four or five years old at this time. *The heads of families, therefore, which were born in Egypt during Jacob's life, seem to have been included.*

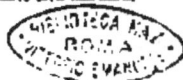

24. The above argument is stated more fully by Kurtz, ii.p.6 :—

(i) 'Hengstenberg has entered thoroughly into an examination of the difficulty referred to, and solves it on the ground that the grandsons and great-grandsons of Jacob, though not yet born, were *in their fathers*, and therefore entered Egypt with them.'

Ans. Why not also the great-great-grandsons, and so on, *ad infinitum?*

(ii) 'Objections have been raised to this interpretation from various quarters: but we must still adhere to it.'

Ans. We *must* adhere to it,' that is, of course, *if* the historical character of the Pentateuch is to be maintained.

(iii) 'The view referred to, which sees in the father the *ensemble* of his descendants, is common to the whole of the Old Testament.'

Ans. But why does the Sacred Writer draw any contrast between the 'three-score and ten persons,' who *went down* to Egypt, and the 'multitude, as the stars of heaven,' who *came out*, since these last, as well as the former, were all in the loins of their father Jacob?

(iv) 'We find it repeatedly in the promises of God to Abraham, Isaac, and Jacob, 'I will give *thee* the land.' 'In *thee* shall all nations of the earth be blessed,' 'Thou shalt be a blessing,' &c.; and in the section before us there are unmistakeable examples of it, 'I will bring *thee* up again,' v.4, evidently not the individual person of Jacob, but his descendants, who were not yet in existence, and of whom Jacob was the one representative.'

Ans. The instances here quoted, where the ancestor is put for the whole race, bear no analogy whatever to the case now before us, where the children are *referred to by name*, as well as the parent.

(v) 'Why, then, should not the same writer, or even another, be able to say, from the same point of view, that the sons of Pharez went down *in* their father to Egypt?'

Ans. Because, from the same point of view, it would be necessary that the children of Reuben's sons, and Simeon's, and Levi's, &c., should all be named and counted in like manner, as being *in* their father, though not yet born.

(vi) 'And just as Joseph's sons, though born in Egypt, are reckoned among the souls who came to Egypt, because in their father they had come thither, so also may these descendants of Jacob, who came to Egypt in their fathers, be regarded as having come with Jacob thither.'

Ans. The narrative lays no stress whatever on the mere fact of their 'coming to' Egypt, in the case of Joseph's sons, as if they had come, because their father had come. The fact of their being born in Egypt, or rather *being* in Egypt, at this time, is all that the writer takes account of; though, wishing to sum up the seventy souls under one category, he uses (inaccurately, as he himself admits) the same expression, 'came into Egypt.' So he sums up, inaccurately, Jacob himself, as one of the 'seventy souls,' among his *children* in v.8,—'These are the names of the children of Israel, which came into Egypt, Jacob *and his sons*.' And he includes him again among the sons of Leah in v.15,—'all the souls of his sons and his daughters * were thirty and three,'—which they would not be without reckoning Jacob, as mentioned in v.8. As to Leah herself, and the other wives of Jacob, it would seem that they are omitted as dead; since in v.5 we read, 'the sons of Israel carried Jacob their father, and their little ones, and their wives,' no mention being made of their *mothers*: and so, too, in v.26, mention is made of 'Jacob's sons' wives,' but not of his own.

25. KURTZ continues his remarks as follows : —

(i) 'The reasons already assigned serve to show that such an explanation is both *admissible* and *necessary*; and the following data heighten its *probability*.'

Ans. It is wholly *inadmissible*, with the passages quoted in (19) before our eyes; and only *necessary*, if the veracity of the Pentateuch must be maintained at all cost, since the historical truth of the whole Mosaic narrative, which in so many places reiterates the statement in question, is seriously involved in its accuracy. It will be seen, presently, that not one of the 'data,' which KURTZ is about to give, tends in any degree to diminish the difficulty.

(ii) 'In the list of the families of Israel, which was prepared in the last year of the journey through the desert, N.xxvi, there are so grandsons of Jacob mentioned besides those named in G.xlvi. It is difficult to explain this, if the arrival in Egypt, spoken of in G.xlvi, is to be taken precisely as a *terminus ad quem*. Are we to suppose, then, that there were no children born to Jacob's sons in the land of Egypt ?'

Ans. Certainly, if the plain meaning of the text of Scripture will not allow us to suppose the contrary. There was, however, Jochebed, the *daughter* of Levi, who is not numbered with the 'seventy souls' in G.xlvi, and whom, it is expressly said, her mother 'bare to Levi *in Egypt*,' N.xxvi.59.

There are also several great-grandsons of Jacob besides those named in G.xlvi, which are mentioned in N.xxvi, as v.8, Eliab, the son of Pallu, v.29, Machir, the son of Manasseh, v.85, Shuthelah, Becher, and Tahan, the sons of Ephraim, Moreover, Zarah, Judah's other son by Tamar, had a son, Zabdi, Jo.vii.1, who is not mentioned in G.xlvi, but appears in 1 Ch.ii.6, under the name of Zimri, with four other sons of Zarah.

(iii) 'In G.xlvi.5, where there is no question of genealogy, and the individuals emigrating are described from a historical point of view, we read not of the

---

* He has named only *one* daughter, Dinah, v.15. But the Hebrew idiom allows of this; thus in v.23 we have 'The *sons* of Dan, Hushim;' and so in v.27 we read of his 'sons' *daughters*,' though only *one* is mentioned, Serah, the daughter of Asher, v.17.

grandchildren of Jacob's sons, but merely of their *children*, who are described as little ones.'

Ans. KURTZ should have written 'but merely of their *little ones*;' for there is nothing said about their being only 'children;' they might be children or grandchildren. If it were necessary to give any further reply to so feeble an argument, we might say that the expression 'little one' is used in G.xliv.20 of Benjamin, when he must have been more than twenty-two years of age, since he was born before Joseph, at seventeen years of age, G.xxxvii.2, was sold into Egypt, and Joseph was now *thirty-nine* (20, note), and he remembered his brother tenderly. In fact, Benjamin had actually, according to the story, ten sons of his own, G.xlvi.21, possibly by more than one wife; and yet he is called a 'little one.' Hence full-grown sons, such as Pharez and Zarah, might be included in the expression 'little ones,' as well as their children. Again, in G.xlvi.7, we read, 'his sons and his sons' sons with him, his daughters and his sons' daughters, ['his daughters and his *daughters*' daughters,' LXX,] and *all his seed*, brought he with him into Egypt.' And, accordingly, in v.17, we have two *grandchildren* of Asher, Heber and Malchiel.

(iv) 'In the case of Hezron and Hamul, the author appears desirous of intimating that they were not born in Canaan, and that he regarded them as substitutes for Er and Onan, who died there. VATABLA has expressed the same opinion. Thus he says: 'It is probable that the sons of Pharez, who were born in Egypt, are mentioned, because they were substituted for the two sons of Judah, who died in Canaan. The historian clearly asserts as much; and, when he adds that the latter died in the land of Canaan, he plainly implies that the sons of Pharez, who were put in their place, had not been born there.''

Ans. But, if Hezron and Hamul are substituted for Er and Onan, for whom are Heber and Malchiel, the sons of Beriah, Asher's son, v.17, supposed to be substituted? And how is it that Hezron and Hamul, the sons of Pharez, are mentioned, and Zaldi and the other sons of Zarah, are not mentioned? Plainly, because the former are supposed to have been born in the land of Canaan, and the latter not.

20. I have quoted at full length the arguments of KURTZ, as being those of one of the best modern defenders of the ordinary view. Their feebleness is itself the strongest proof of the unsoundness of his position. Nothing, indeed, has more tended to convince my own mind of the hollowness of the cause which he advocates, than the efforts made by himself and HENGSTENBERG, in this and other instances, (as we shall see hereafter,) to force the text of Scripture to say what it plainly does not say, in order to get rid of a palpable contradiction. At the

same time, I gladly pay a tribute of respect to the ability and
candour, with which KURTZ generally writes. In respect of the
latter quality he contrasts very favourably with some other
writers on both sides of the question.[*]

27. It may be well, however, to quote here the exact words
of HENGSTENBERG, *Pent.*ii.289-294, with reference to the
question now before us, that so the reader may be able to judge
for himself as to the correctness of the above statements   It will
be seen that most of his arguments have been reproduced by
KURTZ, and have been already disposed of. The others probably
appeared to KURTZ himself to be too weak to deserve a notice.

'The following reasons may be assigned for believing that the author did not
intend to name only those who were born at the time of going down into Egypt.

(i) 'Reuben, when Jacob's sons wished to take their last journey to Egypt, had
no more than *two* sons This is evident from xlii.37, 'Slay my *two* sons, if I
bring him not to thee.' If he had had several, he would have made the offer of
several. But, in xlvi.9, *four* sons of Reuben are enumerated. Two of them must,
therefore, have been born in Egypt.'

Ans. This is quite in HENGSTENBERG's style,—'two *must* (not *might*) have been
born in Egypt.' But Reuben's words were spoken when they had returned from
Egypt the first time, not when they were about to go down the second time, xliii.2.
A whole year appears to have elapsed, according to the story, between the first
journey and the second, xlv.6; and, after that, some time elapsed before Jacob

[*] For instance, I do not remember to have met with in KURTZ anywhere a sweep-
ing charge, *of dishonest concealment of the truth*, made against his opponents
generally, as in the following passage of HENGSTENBERG, ii.432.

'From the rationalistic expositors no correction of this error could be *expected*,
since they had an *interest* in not noticing it. *Excepting on account of this interest,*
it is scarcely explicable how such men as GESENIUS and DE WETTE could act as if
this false interpretation were the only possible and existing one.'

The error in question is the retaining the translation 'lend' in Exii.36, which,
according to H., means 'give:' the Israelites 'asked,' not 'borrowed,' of the
Egyptians, and the Egyptians 'gave,' not 'lent,' their jewels. Whether he is
right or wrong in this criticism, it is one, he admits, which is opposed to the
rendering of the LXX, JEROME, LUTHER, CALVIN, as well as to that of ABEN-EZRA,
PHILO, and other ancient Jews. It is surely conceivable that GESENIUS and DE
WETTE may have adhered to the usual translation, not from a dishonest purpose, but
because they thought it the true one.

went down to Egypt. At all events, the interval between the time of Reuben's speech, and that of Jacob's migration, was quite long enough for two more sons to have been born to Reuben in the land of Canaan.

(ii) 'The representation of Benjamin as a youth is so fixed and constant, that it could not enter the thoughts of an Israelite, that, on his going down into Egypt, he had ten sons: comp. xliii.8, xliv.30,31,33, where he is called נַעַר, and xliii.29, where Joseph calls him his son.'

Ans. We have shown above (25, iii) that Benjamin, though called a 'youth,' was more than twenty-two years old, according to the story, at the time of Jacob's migration. It is, therefore, quite possible that he may have had ten sons, —perhaps, by several wives.

(iii) 'The author appears specially to indicate, respecting Hezron and Hamul, that they were a kind of compensation for Er and Onan, and that they were not born in the land of Canaan: comp. v.12, 'But Er and Onan died in the land of Canaan, and the sons of Phares were Hezron and Hamul.''

Ans. The author indicates merely that Er and Onan, though sons of Judah, were not to be numbered with those who went down into Egypt.

(iv) 'Immediately before the genealogy, it is said, xlvi.5, 'And the sons of Israel carried Jacob their father, and their little ones, in the wagons.' Also, according to xliii.8, the family consisted of Jacob, his sons, and their little ones —'both we, and thou, and also our little ones.' But, in the genealogy, Jacob's grandchildren are mentioned as having children. It cannot, therefore, have been the author's design to restrict himself exactly to the point of time, when the children of Israel entered Egypt.'

Ans. We have answered this above in (25, iii). But we may add also, why are not the children named of *all* Jacob's grandchildren, as well as those of Phares and Beriah, except that the latter only are intended to be understood as born in the land of Canaan?

(v) 'In N.xxvi, not a single grandson of Jacob is mentioned besides those whose names are given in G.xlvi. But this can hardly be explained, if in G.xlvi the going down into Egypt is taken precisely as the *terminus ad quem.* Were no other sons born to Jacob's sons in Egypt?'

Answered above in (25, li).

(vi) 'The author, in G.xxxvii.2, announces the 'genealogy (E.V. generations) of Jacob.' The sons of Jacob had been already enumerated in the genealogy of Isaac. It still remained for him to mention the sons' sons, and perhaps some of their grandsons, who had obtained peculiar importance. If the author wished to fulfil the promise given in xxxvii.2, he would not take notice of the accidental circumstance whether the sons' sons were born in Canaan or not, but would exhibit them all fully. Besides, a second genealogical review must follow on the increase, which the family of Jacob would receive in Egypt. But such a one is not extant. At the same time, the author, if he had cut off everything which was subsequent to the going down into

Egypt, would have injured the genealogical plan, which he had constantly followed from the beginning of his work, and which had been already marked as regulating the whole by the subscription, 'This is the genealogy, &c.''

Ans. We can only meet this 'special pleading' with the plain language of the Scripture, xlvi.26,—'All the souls, that came *with Jacob into Egypt*, which came out of his loins, were threescore and six.'

26. Hengstenberg then proceeds as follows : —

'These are the arguments to prove that it could not have been the design of the author merely to name those individuals who were born at the going down into Egypt. Thus supported, we say, with Hartmann, 'what then?' This catalogue is the list of all the males of the family of Jacob, which were born either in Mesopotamia, or in Canaan, or in Egypt, and who either died without heirs, or were made the heads or chiefs of the families of the posterity of Jacob, as appears abundantly from N.xxvi.5. Which, however, of his sons' sons were born in Canaan, and which, besides the sons of Joseph, in Egypt, we are not told in G.xlvi.

'But, against this result, the express declaration of the author himself appears to militate. When in v.26 he says, 'All the souls, that came with Jacob into Egypt, which came out of his loins, besides Jacob's sons' wives, all the souls were threescore and six,' he seems as decidedly as possible to exclude the view that we have advocated. According to it, also, it seems that the contrast made, v.26,27, between the souls who came to or with Jacob into Egypt on the one hand, and Joseph and his sons on the other, is not to be explained.

'We maintain, however, that the appearance here is deceptive,—that the author regarded those, who were born in Egypt, as coming in the person of their fathers with Jacob into Egypt. Our justification of this opinion, by which the contrast between v.26,27, will remain complete, is supported by the following reasons.

(l) 'It is said in v.27, 'All the souls of the house of Jacob, which came into Egypt, were seventy.' Now, since here Joseph's sons are numbered with the souls which came down to Egypt, because they, although born in Egypt, yet came in their father thither, with equal propriety, among the souls which came with Jacob into Egypt might those grandchildren of Jacob be reckoned, who came thither in their fathers. This reason is irrefragable.'

Ans. But evidently the sons of Joseph are not reckoned with those who went down into Egypt with Jacob, because they 'went down in their father,' but because they were born there, or, rather, were *living* there, were 'in Egypt already,' at the time of Jacob's migration.' The description is, of course, literally incorrect ; but the writer's meaning is obvious enough. He wishes to specify all those, 'out of the loins of Jacob,' who were living at the time of the commencement of the sojourn of the Israelites in Egypt, and from whom such a multitude had sprung at the time of the Exodus. Otherwise, as said above, why has he mentioned grandchildren only of Judah and Asher, and not of the other sons of Jacob, as, for instance, the grandsons of Levi ? In point of fact, in the writer's view, Joseph himself had not 'gone down' into Egypt till his father went. He had been carried down as a captive many years before: but from this time dates his true migration into Egypt, when his father settled there, and he and his sons shared in 'the sojourning of the children of Israel.'

(ii) ' v.15 deserves to be noticed; 'These be the sons of Leah, which she bare unto Jacob in Padan-Aram, with her daughter Dinah: all the souls of his sons and his daughters were thirty-three.' By the term 'sons,' here and in v.8, we may either understand sons in a strict sense, or admit that it is used in a wider signification. In both cases the sons appear as appurtenances of their fathers, as in them already existing and born. The same remark applies to v.18, — 'These are the sons of Zilpah, whom Laban gave unto Leah his daughter; and these she bare unto Jacob, sixteen souls.' '

(iii) ' In D.x.22, — 'Thy fathers went down into Egypt with threescore and ten persons,' — Joseph's sons, at all events, are considered as having come down in their father to Egypt.'

(iv) ' This mode of viewing family connections, so foreign to our notions, may be easily detected in a multitude of other places, especially in Genesis. We only refer to the instance in xlvi.4, 'I will go down with thee into Egypt, and I will also surely bring thee up again.' '

Ans. The above three arguments seem to need no reply beyond what has been already given in (24).

' But, it may be asked, if the author gave the names of others, besides those who were already born when Jacob went down into Egypt, how was it that, not content with naming them, he also states their number? When he states the aggregate of Jacob's family to be 'seventy souls,' it seems to indicate that all the persons named were already born.

' We reply, the author's object in making this computation is to show from how small a quantity of seed so rich a harvest was produced. This we learn from E.i.6, 'And all the souls that came out of the loins of Jacob were seventy souls.' and v.7, 'The children of Israel were fruitful, and increased abundantly, and multiplied, and waxed exceeding mighty, and the land was filled with them;' also from D.x.22, 'Thy fathers went down into Egypt with threescore and ten persons; and now Jehovah thy God hath made thee as the stars of heaven for multitude.' A counterpart to this enumeration is the account of the number of Israel at the departure from Egypt in N.i, and before their entrance into Canaan in N.xxvi. Here is the seed, — there the harvest.

' For this object it was perfectly indifferent to the author, whether the numbers were 40, 50, 60, or 70. The contrast between these numbers and the hundreds of thousands remains the same. The author, who must be measured by the standard of a sacred historian (!), not of a writer on statistics, could hence follow his theological principle, which recommended to him the choice of the number seventy. Seven is the signature of the covenant relation between God and Israel, the special theocratic number. By fixing on the covenant number, the author intimated that the increase was the covenant *blessing* (!).

'The number 70 itself leads to the conjecture that some members were either left out or interpolated. If the author's aim had not been to complete the number, he could not, in contradiction to the principle which he elsewhere always follows, have included Dinah and Serah, the latter of whom had no more right than all the rest of Jacob's female grandchildren to a place in the genealogy. That he did this, and inserted a number of the members of the family who were born in Egypt, is accounted for on the same principle. Similar modes of computation are found in other parts of Holy Writ, as in Matt.i.17.'

Ans. Surely, if the author only needed extra names to fill up the number seventy, he would have inserted two of the sons of Zarah rather than the two females, Dinah and Serah.

29. It is painful to mark the shifts, to which so eminent an author has had recourse, in order to avoid confessing the manifest truth in this matter. Of course, if a writer sets out with the determination to maintain at all costs the 'Veracity and Authenticity' of every portion of the Pentateuch, something *must* be said in order, if possible, to dispose of such contradictions as those which we are here considering. I have given the above at full length, as a sample of the manner in which HENGSTENBERG, who is represented as one of the greatest modern champions of the ordinary view, attempts to set aside the plain meaning of the Scripture. In a multitude of other cases, his arguments will be found upon examination to be just as feeble and unsatisfactory as the above, as will more fully appear by the references we shall make to his book in the course of this work. It would answer, however, no useful purpose to quote continually from him, as we have just done, *in extenso.* But the reader may depend on no single argument of his being omitted, which may seem to me for any reason worth noticing, in the progress of our enquiry; and his work, which may be found in an English translation in 'Clark's Theological Library,' is easily accessible to any one.

30. POOL comments as follows:—

'Hezron and Hamul, *though they seem to have been born in Egypt,* yet are here set down amongst those who came into Egypt, because they came hither in their

father's loins, as Levi is said to 'pay tithes in Abraham.' And the children may
as well be said to come thither in their parents, as their father Jacob is said to
return from thence, *v.4*, in his children. *Object.* If this be the sense, why
should these two be mentioned rather than the grandchildren of the other
brethren, who came into Egypt in the same manner? *Ans.* This may be done
either (i) From some special excellency or eminency in them above the rest, as
Hezron was eminent for being the progenitor of the Messiah, and Hamul might
be so for some other cause, though unknown to us; or (ii) Because they were the
first grandchildren that were born in Egypt, and, it may be, *all that were born
there while Jacob lived there*, and therefore are not unfitly named with Jacob, and
allotted to him; as Joseph's two eldest sons, Ephraim and Manasseh, were by
Jacob appropriated to himself, and reckoned as his immediate sons, when all the
rest of Joseph's sons were excluded from that privilege, G.xlviii.5,6. And the
like may be said of the other two grandchildren mentioned *v.17*.'

Ans. Since Jacob lived 17 years in Egypt, G.xlvii.28, Judah was 59 years old,
according to the story (20), at the time of his father's death. Hence, if he was
only 20 years old (20.i.) at his first marriage, he must have been about 24 at the
birth of his third son, and 39, at least, if we suppose that son to have arrived at
maturity at the early age of 15. Thus only 20 years of Judah's life would remain, even on this supposition (which, however, the texts quoted in (19) will not
allow), for Judah to marry again, and to have two *grandsons* born to him by this
second marriage.

It has been suggested also that 'the substantive verb, *which in such sentences
is never introduced but with emphasis*, stands at the head of the clause (וַיִּהְיוּ)—
'and the sons of Pharez, *were* Hezron and Hamul' — this being the only
instance in the enumeration, where it is so employed.' It is thought that 'this
surely marks a distinction,' and implies that 'the sacred historian deliberately
intended to except these two names from the remainder of his list.'

Ans. (i) Whoever will accept the above explanation must explain, as before,
why these two grandsons of Judah are included, together with the two grandsons
of Asher, v.17, among those who 'went down with Jacob into Egypt,' whereas no
other of the great-grandsons of Jacob are mentioned in the list. This surely indicates that these four, and these only, were supposed to have been born before the
descent into Egypt.

(ii) The same substantive verb, וַיִּהְיוּ, occurs in exactly the same way, 'standing
at the head of the clause,' but without any particular 'emphasis,' in N.iii.17,
'and these were the sons of Levi by their names, Gershon, and Kohath, and
Merari.'

(iii) Possibly, the introduction of the substantive verb in the case before us may
have arisen from the interruption in the narrative, caused by the parenthesis,
'but Er and Onan died in the land of Canaan.'

CHAPTER IV.

31. *And Jehovah spake unto Moses, saying, . . . Gather thou
all the Congregation together unto the door of the Tabernacle
of the Congregation. And Moses did as Jehovah commanded
him. And the Assembly was gathered together unto the door
of the Tabernacle of the Congregation.* L.viii.1–4.

First, it appears to be certain that by the expressions used so
often, here and elsewhere, 'the Assembly,' 'the whole Assembly,'
'all the Congregation,' is meant the whole body of the people
— at all events, the *adult males in the prime of life* among
them — and not merely the *elders* or *heads of the people*, as
some have supposed, in order to escape from such difficulties as
that which we are now about to consider. At any rate, I cannot,
with due regard to the truth, allow myself to believe, or attempt
to persuade others to believe, that such expressions as the above
can possibly be meant to be understood of the elders only.

32. We read, for instance, with reference to the Passover,
'The *whole Assembly* of the Congregation of Israel shall kill it
in the evening,' E.xii.6; and again, 'The *whole Congregation*
of the children of Israel murmured against Moses and Aaron
in the wilderness; and the children of Israel said unto them,
. . . Ye have brought us forth into this wilderness, to kill
this *whole Assembly* with hunger.' E.xvi.2,3. And 'Moses
and Aaron fell on their faces before *all the Assembly* of the
Congregation of the children of Israel.' N.xiv.5. And, when

the people were numbered, they 'assembled *all the Congregation* together, and they declared their pedigrees, after their families, by the house of their fathers.' N.i.18.   So '*all the Congregation*' stoned the blasphemer, L.xxiv.14, and the sabbath-breaker, N.xv.36.   So, too, Korah '*gathered all the Congregation* against Moses and Aaron, unto the door of the Tabernacle of the Congregation; and the glory of Jehovah appeared unto *all the Congregation.* . . . . And Moses rose up, and went unto Dathan and Abiram, and the *elders of Israel* followed him,' N.xvi.19,25,—where the ' elders' are plainly distinguished from 'all the Congregation.'   And, when the plague broke out, we are told, ' Aaron took as Moses commanded, and ran into the midst of the *Congregation,* and, behold, the plague was begun among the people.' N.xvi.47.   And, 'When thou shalt blow with them (the two trumpets) *all the Assembly* shall assemble themselves to thee at the door of the Tabernacle of the Congregation; and, if thou blow but with one trumpet, then the *princes,* which are heads of the thousands of Israel, shall gather themselves unto thee.' N.x.3,4.   And once more, 'There was not a word of all which Moses commanded, which Joshua read not before *all the Congregation* of Israel, with the *women,* and the *little ones,* and the *strangers* that were conversant among them.' Jo.viii.35.

33. From some of the above passages, indeed, it might be reasonably inferred, that the *women* also and *children* would be included in the ' whole Congregation.'   For we cannot suppose that these were exempt from death, when the plague broke out 'in the Congregation.'   At all events, it follows distinctly from the last passage that the *old men* must be considered to be included in it.   But let us confine our attention for the present to the 603,550 warriors, N.ii.32, who certainly must have formed a part of 'the whole Congregation,' leaving out of consideration the multitude of old men, women, and children.

34. This vast body of people, then, received on this occasion, and on other similar occasions, as we are told, an express command from Jehovah Himself, to assemble 'at the door of the Tabernacle of the Congregation.' We need not press the word 'all,' so as to include every individual man of this number. Still the expression, 'all the Congregation,' the 'whole Assembly,' must be surely understood to imply the *main body* of those who were able to attend, especially when summoned thus solemnly by the direct voice of Jehovah Himself. The *mass* of these 603,550 men *ought*, we must believe, to have obeyed such a command, and hastened to present themselves at the 'door of the Tabernacle of the Congregation.'

35. As the text says distinctly ' at the door of the Tabernacle,' they must have come *within the Court*. And this, indeed, was necessary for the purpose for which they were summoned on this occasion, namely, to witness the ceremony of the consecration of Aaron and his sons to the Priestly office. This was to be performed inside the Tabernacle itself, and could only, therefore, be seen by those standing at the door.

36. Now the whole width of the *Tabernacle* was 10 cubits or 18 feet, reckoning the cubit at 1·824 ft. (see *Bagster's Bible*), and its length was 30 cubits or 54 feet, as may be gathered from E.xxvi. (Horne's *Introd.* iii.p.232.) Allowing two feet in width for each full-grown man, nine men could just have stood in front of it. Supposing, then, that 'all the Congregation' of adult males in the prime of life had given due heed to the Divine Summons, and had hastened to take their stand, side by side, as closely as possible, in front, not merely of the *door*, but of the whole *end* of the Tabernacle, in which the door was, they would have reached, allowing 18 inches between each rank of nine men, for a distance of more than 100,000 feet,—in fact, nearly *twenty miles!*

37. Further, the *Court* was 100 cubits in length and 50 cubits in breadth, E.xxvii.18, that is, it was about 180 feet long

D

and 90 feet broad. And, since the length of the Tabernacle, as above, was 54 feet, we have for the space left between the Tabernacle and the hangings of the Court, before and behind, 126 feet, that is, 63 feet in front and 63 feet behind, or, perhaps, we may say, 84 feet in front and 42 feet behind. Thus, then, 84 feet would represent that portion of the men in the prime of life, who could by any possibility have been crowded inside the Court in front of the Tabernacle, while the whole body would be represented by 100,000 feet! Or, if we suppose them to fill the *whole width* of the Court, 90 feet, instead of merely the space directly in front of the Tabernacle, 18 feet, still the whole body would extend to a distance of 6,706 yards, nearly *four miles*; whereas that portion of them, who could find any room to stand in front of the Tabernacle, filling up the whole width of the Court, would be represented by 84 feet or 28 yards!

38. But how many would the *whole Court* have contained? Its area (60 yards by 30 yards) was 1800 square yards, and the area of the Tabernacle itself (18 yards by 6 yards) was 108 square yards. Hence the area of the Court outside the Tabernacle was 1692 square yards. But the 'whole Congregation' would have made a body of people, nearly 20 miles — or, more accurately, 33,530 yards — long, and 18 feet or 6 yards wide; that is to say, packed closely together, they would have covered an area of 201,180 square yards. In fact, the Court, when thronged, could only have held 5000 people; whereas the able-bodied men alone exceeded 600,000. Even the ministering Levites, 'from thirty to fifty years old,' were 8,580 in number, N.iv.48; only 504 of these could have stood within the Court in front of the Tabernacle, and not two-thirds of them could have entered the Court, if they had filled it from one end to the other. It is inconceivable how, under such circumstances, 'all the Assembly,' the 'whole Congregation,' could have been summoned to attend 'at the door of the Tabernacle,' by the express command of Almighty God.

CHAPTER V.

39. *These be the words which Moses spake unto all Israel.*
D.i.1.
And Moses called all Israel, and said unto them. D.v.1.
And afterward he read all the words of the Law, the blessings and the curseings, according to all that which is written in the Book of the Law. There was not a word of all that Moses commanded, which Joshua read not before all the Congregation of Israel, with the women, and the little ones, and the strangers that were conversant among them. Jo.viii.34,35.

We have just seen that the men in the prime of life, 'above twenty years of age,' N.i.3, were more than 600,000 in number. We may reckon that the women in the prime of life were about as many, the males under twenty years, 300,000, the females under twenty years, 300,000, and the old people, male and female together, 200,000, making the whole number about two millions. This number, which KURTZ adopts, iii.p.149, is, indeed, a very moderate estimate. In HORNE's *Introd.* iii.p.205, they are reckoned to have formed 'an aggregate of upwards of three millions.'

KALISCH, *Exod.p.*ii, reckons them at 2,500,000. And he adds, p.160: —

A similar proportion is stated by CÆSAR, *Bell. Gall.* i.29, concerning the Helvetii, who numbered 92,000 men capable of bearing arms, whilst their whole population, 'including children, old men, and women,' amounted to 368,000 souls, or exactly four times the former number.

D 2

KITTO says, *Hist. of the Jews, p.*174 : —

As this prime class of the community (the able-bodied men) is usually in the proportion of one-fourth of the whole population, the result would give nearly two millions and a half as the number of the posterity of Jacob.

And he adds, *p.*334 : —

To the 600,000 men we must allow an equal number of females, making 1,200,000; and then we must double that number, to include the males and females under twenty years of age, which are generally found to form about one half of any population. There are circumstances, which show that this estimate cannot be above the truth, and is very probably under.

And so also ROBINSON says, *Bibl. Res, i.p.*74 : —

The whole number, probably, amounted to two and a half millions, and certainly to not less than two millions.

40. The Rev. T. SCOTT remarks : —

The Psalmist informs us, that 'there was not one feeble person among their tribes.' This was a very extraordinary circumstance, which the history of the world cannot parallel. Yet it was very suitable to the situation of those, who had sufficient encumbrances in their march, without having invalids to take care of. It also completed their triumph over Pharaoh and the Egyptians, since they were not constrained to leave one of the company behind them.

It would, indeed, have been an 'extraordinary circumstance,' and without a parallel in the history of mankind, if a mixed community like this could muster 600,000 men fit for war, and yet not contain one single infant, or young child, or pregnant woman, or aged person, or invalid! But, however this may be, SCOTT himself says (note on E.xii.37), 'the whole company could not be much less than two millions.' In short, for *general* purposes, we may fairly compare the whole body of Israelites, together with the 'mixed multitude,' E.xii.38, to the entire population of the city of LONDON, which was 2,362,236, by the census of 1851, increased to 2,803,035, by that of 1861.

41. How, then, is it conceivable that a man should do what Joshua is here said to have done, unless, indeed, the reading every 'word of all that Moses commanded,' with 'the blessings and

cursings, according to all that is written in the book of the Law,' was a mere dumb show, without the least idea of those most solemn words being *heard* by those to whom they were addressed? For, surely, no human voice, unless strengthened by a miracle of which the Scripture tells us nothing, could have reached the ears of a crowded mass of people, as large as the whole population of LONDON. The very crying of the 'little ones,' who are expressly stated to have been present, must have sufficed to drown the sounds at a few yards' distance.

42. It may be said, indeed, that only a portion of this great host was really present, though 'all Israel' is spoken of. And this might have been allowed without derogating from the general historical value of the book, though, of course, not without impeaching the *literal* accuracy of the Scripture narrative, which by some is so strenuously maintained. But the words above quoted from Joshua are so comprehensive, that they will not allow of this. We must suppose that, at least, the great body of the Congregation was present, and not only present, but able to hear the words of awful moment which Joshua addressed to them. Nor can it be supposed that he read them first to one party, and then to another, &c., till 'all the Congregation' had heard them. The day would not have sufficed for reading in this way 'all the blessings and the cursings' in D.xxvii,xxviii,— much less 'all the words of the Law,'—many times over, especially after that he had been already engaged, as the story implies, on the very same day, in writing 'a copy of the Law of Moses' upon the stones set up in Mount Ebal, Jo.viii.32,33. In short, while it is conceivable that a later writer, *imagining* such a scene as this, may have employed such exaggerated terms in describing it, it seems impossible that an *actual eye-witness*, as Moses himself in the one instance or Joshua in the other, *with the real facts of the case before him*, should have expressed himself in such extravagant language.

CHAPTER VI.

43. *And the skin of the bullock, and all his flesh, with his
head, and with his legs, and his inwards, and his dung, even
the whole bullock, shall he (the Priest) carry forth without the
Camp, unto a clean place, where the ashes are poured out,
and burn him on the wood with fire. Where the ashes are
poured out, there shall he be burnt.* L.iv.11,12.

*And the Priest shall put on his linen garment, and his
linen breeches shall he put upon his flesh, and take up the ashes
which the fire hath consumed with the burnt offering on the
Altar, and he shall put them beside the Altar. And he shall
put off his garments, and put on other garments, and carry
forth the ashes without the camp unto a clean place.* L.vi.10,11.

We have seen (39) that the whole population of Israel at the
Exodus may be reckoned at two millions. Now we cannot well
allow for a *living* man, with room for his cooking, sleeping, and
other necessaries and conveniences of life, less than three or
four times the space required for a *dead* one in his grave. And
even then the different ages and sexes would be very disagree-
ably crowded together. Let us allow, however, for each person
on the average three times 6 feet by 2 feet, the size of a coffin
for a full-grown man, — that is, let us allow for each person 36
square feet or 4 square yards. Then it follows that for two
millions of people, (without making any allowance for the
Tabernacle itself, and its Court, and the 44,000 Levites, male

and female N.iii.39, 'who pitched round about it,' N.i.53,)
the Camp must have covered, the people being crowded as
thickly as possible, an area of 8,000,000 square yards, or more
than 1652 acres of ground.

44. Upon this very moderate estimate, then, (which in truth
is far within the mark,) we must imagine a vast encampment of
this extent, swarming with people, more than *a mile and a
half across* in each direction, with the Tabernacle in the
centre; and so says JOSEPHUS, *Ant.iii.*12,5 : —

It was like a well-appointed market; and everything was there ready for sale in
due order; and all sorts of artificers were in the shops; and it resembled nothing
so much as a city, that sometimes was moveable and sometimes was fixed.

Thus the refuse of these sacrifices would have had to be
carried by the Priest himself, (Aaron, Eleazar, or Ithamar, —
there were no others,) a distance of three-quarters of a mile.
It is plain, from the second of the passages above quoted, that the
Priest himself in person was to do this; there is here no room for
the application of the principle, *qui facit per alium, facit per se.*
From the outside also of this great Camp, wood and water would
have had to be fetched for all purposes, if, indeed, such supplies
of wood or water, for the wants of such a multitude as this, could
have been found at all in the wilderness, — under Sinai, for instance, where they are said to have encamped for nearly twelve
months together. How much wood would remain in such a
neighbourhood, after a month's consumption of the city of
LONDON, even at midsummer? And the 'ashes' of the whole
Camp, with the rubbish and filth of every kind, for a population
like that of LONDON, would have had to be carried out in like
manner, through the midst of the crowded mass of people. They
could not surely all have gone outside the Camp for the necessities
of nature, as commanded in D.xxiii.12-14. There were the
aged and infirm, women in childbirth, sick persons, and young
children, who could not have done this. And, indeed, the command itself supposes the person to have a 'paddle' upon his

'weapon,' and, therefore, must be understood to apply only to the *males*, or, rather, only to the 600,000 *warriors*. But the very fact, that this direction for ensuring cleanliness,—'for Jehovah thy God walketh in the midst of thy Camp; therefore shall thy Camp be holy; that He see no unclean thing in thee, and turn away from thee,'—would have been so limited in its application, is itself a very convincing proof of the unhistorical character of the whole narrative.

45. But how huge does this difficulty become, if, instead of taking the excessively cramped area of 1652 acres, less than *three square miles*, for such a Camp as this, we take the more reasonable allowance of Scott, who says 'this encampment is computed to have formed a moveable city of *twelve miles square*,' that is, about the size of LONDON itself,—as it might well be, considering that the population was as large as that of LONDON, and that in the Hebrew tents there were no first, second, third, and fourth stories, no crowded garrets and underground cellars. In that case, the offal of these sacrifices would have had to be carried by Aaron himself, or one of his sons, a distance of six miles ; and the same difficulty would have attended each of the other transactions above-mentioned. In fact, we have to imagine the Priest having himself to carry, on his back on foot, from St. Paul's to the outskirts of the Metropolis, the 'skin, and flesh, and head, and legs, and inwards, and dung, even the whole bullock,' and the people having to carry out their rubbish in like manner, and bring in their daily supplies of water and fuel, after first cutting down the latter where they could find it ! Further, we have to imagine half a million of men going out daily — the 22,000 Levites for a distance of *six miles* — to the suburbs for the common necessities of nature ! The supposition involves, of course, an absurdity. But it is our duty to look plain facts in the face.

CHAPTER VII.

46. *And Jehovah spake unto Moses, saying, When thou
takest the sum of the children of Israel after their number, then
shall they give every man a ransom for his soul unto Jehovah
when thou numberest them, that there be no plague among
them when thou numberest them. This they shall give, every
one that passeth among them that are numbered, half a shekel
after the shekel of the Sanctuary; an half shekel shall be the
offering of Jehovah.* E.xxx.11-13.

We may first notice in passing, that the expression, 'shekel
of the Sanctuary,' in the above passage, could hardly have been
used in this way until there *was* a Sanctuary in existence, or,
rather, until the Sanctuary had been *some time* in existence, and
such a phrase had become *familiar* in the mouths of the
people. Whereas here it is put into the mouth of Jehovah,
speaking to Moses on Mount Sinai, six or seven months before
the Tabernacle was made. And in E.xxxviii.24,25,26, we have
the same phrase used again, of the actual contributions of the
people *towards the building of the Sanctuary.*

The LXX, indeed, render the Hebrew phrase by τὸ δίδραχμον
τὸ ἄγιον, 'the sacred shekel.' But this can hardly be the true
meaning of the original, שֶׁקֶל הַקֹּדֶשׁ; and, if it were, the difficulty would still remain, to explain what the 'sacred shekel'
could mean, before any sacred system was established.

47. But these words direct that, whenever a numbering of the

people shall take place, each one that is numbered shall pay a
'ransom for his soul,' of half a shekel. Now in E.xxxviii.26
we read of such a tribute being paid, 'a bekah for every man,
that is, half a shekel after the shekel of the Sanctuary, for every
one that went to be numbered, from twenty years old and
upward,' that is, the *atonement-money* is collected; but nothing
is there said of any *census* being taken. On the other hand, in
N.i.1–46, more than six months after the date of the former
occasion, we have an account of a very formal numbering of the
people, the result being given for each particular tribe, and the
total number summed up at the end ; here the *census* is made,
but there is no indication of any *atonement-money* being paid,
The omission in each case might be considered, of course, as
accidental, it being supposed that, in the first instance, the numbering really took place, and in the second the tribute was paid,
though neither circumstance is mentioned.

But then it is surprising that the number of adult males
should have been *identically the same* (603,550) *on the first
occasion as it was half a year afterwards.*

48. KURTZ remarks upon this matter as follows, iii.*p*.20 : —

There is something striking in the fact, that the census, which was taken now,
gave precisely the same result as the poll-tax, which was levied at the commencement of the erection of the Tabernacle about half a year before. J. D. MICHAELIS
solves the difficulty in the following manner: 'In E.xxxviii,' he says, 'there is
no account of an actual numbering; but every one, who was more than twenty
years old, paid his tax, and was registered accordingly. But on the present occasion Moses received instructions to arrange the lists and sum them up. N.i.li.
The names had been given in *before*, though the actual counting only took place
now. And, therefore, Moses did not hesitate, when recording the account of the
tax, to insert what were afterwards found to be the actual numbers.' But there is
no intimation whatever of the names being registered, when the tax was levied,
and in itself it does not appear to be at all a probable thing. If the numbers in
both instances are founded upon one and the same census, which we also regard as
probably the case, we must look for the census in question, not to E.xxxviii, but
to N.i. We are shut up to this by the solemnity and formality, with which the
census in N.i was commanded, organised, and carried out. In E.xxxviii we have
simply the raising of a tax, and no numbering at all. And, as the increase or de-
crease in the number of the people must have been very trifling in the brief space

of six or seven months, the result might be employed without hesitation, in giving the amount which the poll-tax yielded.

49. To which we must reply as follows :—

(i) Is there any reasonable ground for supposing that the number of those, who contributed the silver for the building of the Sanctuary, would not have been noted and remembered as accurately as that of those of whom the census was taken ?

(ii) Why should the amount of *silver* in E.xxxviii.25 be less accurate than that of the *gold* in v.21, or the *brass* in v.29 ?

(iii) In fact the amount is *checked*, as it were, and verified in the case of the silver, by the same statement being repeated in E.xxxviii in three different forms. In v.25 the sum of the silver paid is reckoned in talents and shekels; in v.26 the number of men is given, by whom it was paid; and in v.27,28, the amount of silver is again stated, the separate portions being specified, which were devoted to different purposes.

(iv) It is plain, therefore, that the story in Exodus purports to be a strictly accurate account of the matter, and not merely a rough, or even a pretty close, estimate, as Kurtz supposes.

(v) Even Kurtz himself is obliged to give up the notion of the literal historical accuracy of *both* accounts.

50. But Kurtz remarks further upon N.i,ii, (ii.p.202).

We are also struck with the fact, that the amount is given in round *hundreds*, in the case of every tribe excepting Gad, and that in this instance the *fifty* is inserted; thus :—

E. Camp, 186,400	Judah,	74,600	W. Camp, 108,100	Ephraim,	40,500
	Issachar,	54,400		Manasseh,	32,200
	Zebulun,	57,400		Benjamin,	35,400
S. Camp, 151,450	Reuben,	46,500	N. Camp, 157,600	Dan,	62,700
	Simeon,	59,300		Asher,	41,500
	Gad,	45,650		Naphtali,	53,400

The idea is hereby suggested that the numbers were taken by *tens*, if not by *fifties*. The judicial classification proposed by Jethro, Ex.xviii.21, was probably taken as the basis. In any case we prefer the conjecture, that there was some such want of precision as this, to the notion expressed by Havernick, who regards the fact that, in the case of every tribe, the result yielded such round numbers as these, as a proof of the special Providence of God. In his opinion, since the supposition of any such inaccuracy as this is incompatible with the care and completeness, which are apparent throughout, and as it could not possibly apply to the case of the Levites, whose numbers must of necessity be given with precision, ' it must be acknowledged that, in this natural neatness in the numbers of the Israelites, we have the evident seal of the care, with which the increase of the nation was superintended by Jehovah.'

51. To which also we reply :—

(i) If Baumgarten's fanciful reason were the true one, it would be strange that the numbers do not come out 'neat' and complete, all in round hundreds or even thousands, like the Levites (22,000, N.iii.39), instead of with an odd fifty, and still more strange that the firstborn should amount to the very unsightly number of 22,273, N.iii.43.

(ii) If they were reckoned by fifties, as Kurtz supposes, it is still strange that the numbers should result in round hundreds for all the tribes except one, and that the same phenomenon should recur on the second numbering, N.xxvi.

(iii) In this second numbering, however, Reuben is an exception to the general rule, and his number is 43,730, c.7. And that the odd 'thirty' here is not a mere clerical error for 'fifty,' is shown by the fact, that the sum of the numbers of all the twelve tribes is added up here as before, c.51, and the sum-total (601,730) requires the 43,730 of Reuben. Hence Kurtz's idea of the census having been taken by fifties falls to the ground completely.

(iv) In fact, as Baumgarten observes, the supposition of any such inaccuracy, as Kurtz suggests, is absolutely incompatible, not only with the 'care and completeness' with which the census was taken, and the exactness required in the case of the Levites, but above all with the fact that, not for every ten or fifty, but for every individual, a 'ransom for his soul' was to be paid at any such numbering.

52. Hävernick explains the matter thus, *Pent.p.306*: —

The census in the first year was required in order to levy the impost for the erection of the Tabernacle; the other, to decide the order of the encampment and march. The latter object did not require a census properly so called. All that was necessary was, to have a review of the tribes; and, as the *former* census was made the *basis*, it is evident that it was only a review of the numbers of each tribe that was designed. It is clear from the text itself that this is no arbitrary opinion. Prominent expression is here given to the fact that the new numbering was made 'after their families, by the house of their fathers,' N.i.2,18. This was the only necessary addition to the first numbering. But, that the latter was made use of, is both probable in itself, and is confirmed by the agreement of the sum total in each (!).

Ans. We can only say, with Kurtz (48), If the numbers in both instances are founded upon one and the same census, we must look for the census in question, not to Exxxviii, but to N.i. Is it conceivable that, if *each individual* was now required to 'declare his pedigree,' N.i.18, the number of the whole body of each tribe should yet have been taken from the *former* census?

As to the 'round numbers,' Hävernick says, *Pent.p.307*,

'Detail was here regarded as being not so important; a general computation of the whole was all that was proposed, and, therefore, Moses gives the more exact number only where something depends upon it; see N.iii.39,43.

Ans. As before, if the pedigree of each individual was registered, it is plain that the sum-total of each tribe must have been taken at the second census, and that of the tribe of Levi is a 'round number,' 22,000, N.iii.39, like the rest.

CHAPTER VIII.

53. *Take ye every man for them which are in his tents.* E.xvi.16.

Here we find that, immediately after their coming out of Egypt, the people were provided with *tents*,—cumbrous articles to have been carried, when they fled out in haste, ' taking their dough before it was leavened, their kneading-troughs being bound up in their clothes upon their shoulders,' E.xii.34. It is true, this statement conflicts strangely with that in L.xxiii. 42,43, where it is assigned as a reason for their 'dwelling in booths' for seven days at the Feast of Tabernacles, ' that your generations may know that I made the children of Israel to dwell in *booths*, when I brought them out of the land of Egypt.' It cannot be said that the word 'booths' here means 'tents'; because the Hebrew word for a *booth*, made of boughs and bushes, הכס, which is the word here used, is quite different from that for a *tent*, להא, used in E.xvi.16. And, besides, in the context of the passage in Leviticus, we have a description of the way in which these booths were to be made. ' Ye shall take you the boughs of goodly trees, branches of palm-trees, and the boughs of thick trees, and willows of the brook,' *v*. 40. This seems to fix the meaning of the Hebrew word in this particular passage, and to show that it is used in its proper sense of 'booths'; though in 2 S.xi.11, and one or two other places, it is also used improperly for 'tents.'

54. There is not, however, the slightest indication in the story that they ever did live in booths, nor is it conceivable when they

46   THE ISRAELITES DWELLING IN TENTS.

could have done so. It is true, we are told that, on the first day,
when they went out of Egypt, they 'journeyed from Rameses to
Succoth,' E.xii.37, where the name Succoth means 'booths.'
But it cannot surely be supposed that, in the hurry and confusion of this flight, they had time to cut down 'boughs and
bushes' to make booths of, if even there were trees from which
to cut them. It has, indeed, been suggested, that in L.xxiii.43,
it should be translated, 'that your generations may know that
I made the children of Israel to dwell in *Succoth*, when I
brought them out of the land of Egypt,'—as if the Feast of
Tabernacles commemorated the *transition stage* from the
Egyptian to the wilderness life, when they had left houses,
but had not yet come to live in hair or skin tents. I cannot
say that this explanation satisfies my own mind. They did not,
surely, *dwell* in Succoth, E.xii.37, xiii.20. But, however this may
be, we are required to believe that *they had tents*, at all events,
as these are repeatedly mentioned ; whereas booths are only
spoken of in this single passage of the book of Leviticus.

54. Now, allowing *ten* persons for each tent, (and decency
would surely require that there should not be more than this,—
a Zulu hut in Natal contains on an average only *three and a
half*,) — two millions of people would require 200,000 tents.
How then did they acquire these ? Had they provided this
enormous number in expectation of marching, when all their
request was to be allowed to go 'for three days into the wilderness,' E.v.3 ? For they were not living in tents in the land
of Egypt, as we gather from the fact, that they were to take of
the blood of the paschal lamb, and 'strike it on the *two side-
posts*, and on the *lintel* or *upper door-post*,' of their houses,
E.xii.7, and none of them was to 'go out *at the door of his
house* until the morning,' v.22.

55. But, further, if they had had these tents, how could they
have *carried* them ? They could not have borne them on their
shoulders, since these were already occupied with other burdens.
And these burdens themselves were by no means insignificant.

For, besides their 'kneading-troughs,' with the dough unleavened, 'bound up in their clothes upon their shoulders,' as
well as all other necessaries for daily domestic use, for sleeping,
cooking, &c., there were the infants and young children, who
could scarcely have gone on foot twenty miles a day as the
story requires; there were the aged and infirm persons, who
must have likewise needed assistance; they must have carried
also those goods of various kinds, which they brought out of
their treasures so plentifully for the making of the Tabernacle;
and, above all this, *they must have taken with them grain or
flour enough for at least a month's use,* since they had no
manna given to them till they came into the wilderness of Sin,
' on the fifteenth day of the second month after their departing
out of the land of Egypt,' E.xvi.1.

57. There were the *cattle* certainly, which might have been
turned to some account for this purpose, if trained to act as
pack-oxen. But then, what a prodigious number of trained oxen
would have been needed to carry these 200,000 tents! One ox
will carry 120 lbs., and a *canvas* tent, 'that will hold *two*
people and a fair quantity of luggage,' weighs from 25 to 40 lbs.
(GALTON's *Art of Travel, pp.*33,177). Of such tents as the above,
with poles, pegs, &c., a single ox might, possibly, carry *four*,
and even this would require 50,000 oxen. But these would be
of the lightest modern material, whereas the Hebrew tents, we
must suppose, were made of *hair*, E.xxvi.7, xxxvi.14, or, rather,
of *skin*, E.xxvi.14, xxxvi.19, and were, therefore, of course, much
heavier. Besides this, these latter were *family* tents, not made
merely for soldiers or travellers, and required to be very much
larger for purposes of common decency and convenience. One
ox, perhaps, might have carried one such a tent, large enough to
accommodate ten persons, with its apparatus of pole and cords:
and thus they would have needed for this purpose 200,000 oxen.
But oxen are not usually trained to carry goods upon their backs
as pack-oxen, and will by no means do so, if untrained.

CHAPTER IX.

58. *The children of Israel went up harnessed out of the land of Egypt.* E.xii.18.

The word םיֻשׁמֲח, which is here rendered 'harnessed,' appears to mean 'armed' or 'in battle array,' in all the other passages where it occurs. Thus, Jo.i.14, 'But ye shall pass before your brethren *armed*, all the mighty men of valour, and help them.' So, Jo.iv.12, 'And the children of Reuben, and the children of Gad, and half the tribe of Manasseh, passed over *armed* before the children of Israel, as Moses spake unto them.' And, Ju.vii.11, 'Then went he down, with Phurah his servant, unto the outside of the armed men that were in the host.' It is possible also that the Hebrew word םישֻׁח, which occurs in N.xxxii.17, and is rendered 'armed' in the English Version, but which GESENIUS derives from שׁוּח, 'to make haste,' and renders 'hastening' or 'in haste,' may be a corruption from םיֻשׁמֲח, by the accidental omission of a letter.

59. It is, however, inconceivable that these down-trodden, oppressed people should have been allowed by Pharaoh to possess arms, so as to turn out at a moment's notice 600,000 armed men. If such a mighty host,—nearly nine times as great as the whole of Wellington's army at Waterloo, (69,686 men, ALISON's *History of Europe*, xix. p.401),—had had arms in their hands, would they not have risen long ago for their liberty, or, at all events, would there have been no danger of their rising? Besides, the warriors formed a distinct caste in Egypt, as

HERODOTUS tells us, ii. 165, 'being in number, when they are most numerous, 160,000, none of whom learn any mechanical art, but apply themselves wholly to military affairs.' Are we to suppose, then, that the Israelites acquired their arms by 'borrowing' on the night of the Exodus? Nothing whatever is said of this, and the idea itself is an extravagant one. But, if even in this, or any other, way they had come to be possessed of arms, is it conceivable that 600,000 armed men, in the prime of life, would have cried out in panic terror, 'sore afraid,' E.xiv.10, when they saw that they were being pursued?

60. The difficulty of believing this has led many commentators to endeavour to explain otherwise, if possible, the meaning of the word. Accordingly, in the margin of the English Bible we find suggested, instead of 'harnessed' or 'armed,' in all the above passages except Jo.iv.12, 'by five in a rank,' because the Hebrew word חֲמֻשִׁים has a resemblance to חָמֵשׁ, 'five.' And others again explain it to mean ' by fifties,' as the five thousand were arranged in the wilderness of Bethsaida, Mark vi.40.

It will be seen at once, however, that these meanings of the word will not at all suit the other passages quoted in (58). And, indeed, by adopting the first of them, we should only get rid of one difficulty to introduce another quite as formidable. For, if 600,000 men marched out of Egypt 'five in a rank,' allowing a yard for marching room between each rank, they must have formed a column 68 miles long, and it would have taken several days to have *started* them all off, instead of their going out all together 'that self-same day,' E.xii.41,42,51. On the second supposition, they might have formed a column seven miles long, which was certainly possible in the open, undulating, desert between Cairo and Suez. But it cannot surely be supposed that the strong, able-bodied, men kept regular ranks, as if marching for war, when they were only hasting out of Egypt, and when their services must have been so much

required for the assistance of the weaker members of their
families, the women and children, the sick, infirm, and aged.

61. It might be thought, indeed, that the Hebrew word may
have been used originally of warriors, with reference to their
marching in ranks of five or fifty, but may here be used in a
metaphorical sense, to express the idea that they went out of
Egypt 'with a high hand,' E.xiv.8, in a spirited and orderly
manner, not as a mere hurrying, confused, rabble. Accordingly,
Scott writes —

The margin intimates that the word translated *harnessed* may signify *by five in
a rank.* But the room, which such a multitude must have taken from the van to
the rear, is immense, had they marched in this manner, as there would have been
120,000 lines of five men each, besides women and children. It seems rather to
mean that they marched *in five distinct squadrons,* or, in general, that though unarmed, they journeyed *in regular order,* and not as a disorderly multitude.

But, as before observed, neither of these meanings will suit the
passages quoted in (58). And, besides, if they did not take it
with them out of Egypt, where did they get the armour, with
which, about a month afterwards, they fought the Amalekites,
E.xvii.8-13, and 'discomfited them with the edge of the
sword'? So, too, shortly afterwards, we find Moses commanding the Levites under Sinai, E.xxxii.27, 'Put every man
his sword by his side, &c.' And, in the second year, we read
of their 'girding on every man his weapons of war,' D.i.41, to
go up and fight with the Amorites.

It may, perhaps, be said that they had stripped the Egyptians,
whom they 'saw lying dead upon the sea-shore,' E.xiv.30. And
so writes Josephus, *Ant.* ii.16.6 : —

On the next day, Moses gathered together the weapons of the Egyptians, which
were brought to the camp of the Hebrews by the current of the sea and the force
of the winds assisting it. And he conjectured that this also happened by Divine
Providence, that so they might not be destitute of weapons.

It is plain that Josephus had perceived the difficulty. The
Bible-story, however, says nothing about this stripping of the
dead, as surely it must have done, if it really took place. And,

though body-armour might have been obtained in this way, would swords, and spears, and shields, in any number, have been washed upon the shore by the waves, or have been retained, still grasped in the hands of drowning men?

62. If, indeed, this were the *only* difficulty in the story of the Exodus, viz. to account for the Israelites possessing a sufficient number of arms for their first fight, some such a solution of it as the above, (by supposing that they stripped the corpses of the Egyptians,) might be admitted as being within the range of possibility, however far-fetched it must seem, more especially when the narrative itself is altogether silent upon the subject. But this, as we have already seen, is only one of many such difficulties. And even this supposition will not do away with the fact, that the stubborn word םישִׁמֻחֲ exists in the text before us. Besides, we must suppose that the *whole body* of 600,000 warriors were armed, when they were numbered, N.i.3, under Sinai. They possessed arms, surely, at that time, according to the story. How did they get them, unless they took them out of Egypt?

63. If, then, the historical veracity of this part of the Pentateuch is to be maintained, we must believe that 600,000 armed men, (though it is inconceivable how they obtained their arms,) had, by reason of their long servitude, become so debased and inhuman in their cowardice, (and yet they fought bravely enough with Amalek a month afterwards,) that they could not strike a single blow for their wives and children, if not for their own lives and liberties, but could only weakly wail, and murmur against Moses, saying, ' It had been better for us to serve the Egyptians, than that we should die in the wilderness,' E.xiv.12.

And so, indeed, KALISCH writes, with what appearance of reason let the reader determine, *Exod.p.*185 : —

As faint reminiscences, and fluctuating traditions from past centuries, were the only bands by which the vast numbers of the Israelites were feebly connected, — as, further, the tyrannical measures of the Pharaohs had perfectly attained their aim

in making the Israelites indifferent and deadened to all higher interests, for this
large population did not even attempt to revolt against their oppressors,—and as
political independence was an idea, which they had neither inherited from their
ancestors, nor had themselves practically acquired,— the miraculous interposition of
God, which, working through the agency of Moses, had effected their release, [by
a succession of stupendous miracles which they had just witnessed, and the last
and most awful of which had been wrought on their behalf only the day before
yesterday!] had only silenced, not extirpated, their doubts and their reluctance.
And now, when they saw themselves in a dreary and trackless wilderness, in which
they must, even under the most favourable circumstances, expect all the horrors of
famine, and when, to complete their consternation, they beheld their mortal enemies
wrathfully follow behind them, and the foaming sea wildly rage before them, was
it not natural that the people, forgetting a feeling of honour, which had as yet
taken no root in their minds, wished longingly to return to the old yoke of servitude, to the miseries and humiliations of which long habit had almost reconciled
them, and in which their daily wants were, at least, tolerably provided for?

64. KURTZ comments on the above passage as follows : —

'According to E.xiii.18, the children of Israel departed from Egypt חֲמֻשִׁים.
The SEPTUAGINT rendering is 'in the fifth generation.' CLERICUS explains it in the
same manner, with special reference to G.xv.16, 'in the fourth generation they
shall come hither again,' and to E.vi.16-20, [where the generation of Moses and
Aaron is given, Jacob, Levi, Kohath, Amram, Moses and Aaron, so that the next generation, that of Eleazar, Joshua, &c., the generation in the prime of life at the time
of the Exodus, was the fifth in descent from Jacob]. FULLER also adheres firmly
to the derivation of the word from חָמֵשׁ, five. But he renders it by quinquedies,
and supposes it to mean that they were drawn up in five columns.

'But neither of these renderings corresponds to the sense in which the word is
used in other places. In N.xxxii.30,32, and in D.iii.18, the very same men who
are called חֲמֻשִׁים in Jo.i.14,vi.12, are described as בֵּני חַיִל, accincti, expediti ad
iter s. ad prelium. The VULGATE translates it armati ; AQUILA, ἐνωπλισμένοι ; SYM-
MACHUS, καθωπλισμένοι. A more suitable rendering of the passages cited would
be ' equipped for battle,' ' in battle array,' which certainly includes the action of
being armed. The etymology is doubtful. GESENIUS refers to the cognate roots, חָמֵן,
acer fuit, חָמֵס, violenter egit, oppressit, and to the kindred word in Arabic, which
means acer, strenuus fuit in prælio.

'It has been objected to our explanation that the Israelites went away unarmed.
But this is nowhere stated; and the panic, which seized them afterwards, does
not prove that they were not armed. On the contrary, we read shortly afterwards of their fighting a regular battle with the Amalekites. There could have
been no reason whatever for dividing the people into five companies. The
SEPTUAGINT rendering has still less to recommend it; because there is no ground
for the assumption, that Moses was the fifth [rather fourth] in order of descent from
Jacob.'

Ans. It will be seen hereafter that Kurtz's reason for objecting to the LXX rendering has no validity. It is sufficient, however, to say, that both this and the other rendering, which he justly rejects, are inadmissible in the other passages where the word is used.

'But the rendering, 'equipped for battle,' or 'in battle array,' furnishes a good, appropriate, and very significant meaning. This was a necessary part of the triumphant and jubilant attitude, in which Israel was to depart from Egypt.'

Ans. This is, no doubt, true. But it involves the extreme improbability of the Israelites being possessed of these arms in the land of Egypt, as well as that of their acting in the way in which they are said to have acted, if they really did possess them.

CHAPTER X.

65. *Then Moses called for all the elders of Israel, and said unto them, Draw out now, and take you a lamb according to your families, and kill the Passover. And ye shall take a bunch of hyssop, and dip it in the blood that is in the bason, and strike the lintel and the two side-posts with the blood that is in the bason; and none of you shall go out at the door of his house until the morning. . . . And the children of Israel went away, and did as Jehovah had commanded Moses and Aaron: so did they.* E.xii.21–28.

That is to say, in *one single day*, the whole immense population of Israel, as large as that of LONDON, was instructed to keep the Passover, and actually did keep it. I have said 'in one single day'; for the first notice of any such Feast to be kept is given in *v.*3 of this very chapter, and we find it written, in *v.*12, 'I will pass through the land of Egypt *this night*, and will smite all the first-born in the land of Egypt, both man and beast.'

It cannot be said that they had notice several days beforehand, for they were to '*take*' the lamb on the tenth day of the month, and '*kill*' it on the fourteenth, *v.*3,6, and so *v.*12 only means to say ' on *that* night — the night of the fourteenth — I will pass through the land of Egypt.' For the expression in *v.*12 is distinctly הזה, '*this*,' not ההוא, '*that*,' as in xiii.8; and so *v.*14, '*this* day shall be unto you for a memorial;' and, besides, in the chapter preceding, xi.4, we read, 'And Moses said [to Pharaoh], Thus saith Jehovah, *about midnight* will I go out into the midst of Egypt, and all the first-born in the land of Egypt shall die,' where there can be no doubt that the 'midnight' then next at hand is intended. It is true that the story, as it now stands, with the directions about 'taking' the lamb on the tenth day, and 'keeping' it till the fourteenth, are perplexing and contradictory. But this is only one of many similar phenomena, which will have to be considered more closely hereafter.

Let us now see what the above statement really implies, when translated into simple every-day matter of fact.

66. 'Moses called for all the elders of Israel.' We must suppose, then, that the 'elders' lived somewhere near at hand. But where did the two millions live? And how could the order, to keep the Passover, have been conveyed, with its minutest particulars, to *each individual household* in this vast community, in one day, — rather, in *twelve hours*, since Moses received the command on the very same day, on which they were to kill the Passover *at even*, E.xii.6 ?

It must be observed that it was absolutely necessary that the notice should be distinctly given to each separate family. For it was a matter of life and death. Upon the due performance of the Divine command it depended whether Jehovah should 'stride across' (חסף) the threshold, (see Is.xxxi.5,) and protect the house from the angel of death, or not. And yet the whole matter was perfectly new to them. The specific directions,— about choosing the lamb, killing it at even, sprinkling its blood, and eating it, with unleavened bread, 'not raw, nor sodden at all with water, but roast with fire,' 'with their loins girded, their shoes on their feet, and their staff in their hand,' — were now for the first time communicated to Moses, by him to the elders, and by them to the people. These directions, therefore, could not have been conveyed by any mere *sign*, intimating that they were now to carry into execution something about which they had been informed before. They must be plainly and fully delivered to each individual head of a family, or to a number of them gathered together; though these, of course, might be ordered to assist in spreading the intelligence to others, but so that no single household should be left uninformed upon the matter.

67. This would, of course, be done *most* easily, if we could suppose that the whole Hebrew community lived as closely together as possible, in one great city. In that case, we should have to imagine a message of this nature, upon which life and death depended, conveyed, without fail, to every single family in a population as large as that of LONDON, between sunrise and sunset, — and that, too, without their having had any previous notice whatever on the subject, and without any preparations having been made beforehand to facilitate such a communication.

68. Further, we are told that 'every woman was to borrow of her neighbour, and of her that sojourned in her house, jewels of silver, and jewels of gold, and raiment,' E.iii.22. From this it would seem to follow that the Hebrews were regarded as living in the midst of the Egyptians, mixed up freely with them in their dwellings. And this appears to be confirmed by the statement, E.xii.35,36, that, when suddenly summoned to depart, they hastened, at a moment's notice, to 'borrow' in all directions from the Egyptians, and collected such a vast amount of treasure, in a very short space of time, that they 'spoiled the Egyptians.' And, indeed, it would seem only natural that those among the Egyptians who did not sympathise with the mad folly of their king, and had all along a friendly feeling, and by this time also a deep respect, for Israel, should have taken refuge in the Hebrew dwellings, and sought immunity in this way from the plagues which ravaged the land. And so writes HENGSTENBERG, i. 409 : —

The Israelites dwelt in houses, and intermixed with Egyptians, so that the destroying angel would pass by one door and stop at another. They lived with the

Egyptians, with whom, in part, they stood on most friendly terms, in cities.
According to E.iii.20-22, it was not unfrequently the case, that Egyptian lodgers
dwelt with an Israelitish householder, and those persons of good property, so that
they could give from abundance gold and silver ornaments and clothes.

69. But the supposition of their borrowing in this way, even
if they lived in such a city, involves prodigious difficulties. For
the city, in that case, could have been no other than Rameses
itself, from which they started, E.xii.87, a 'treasure-city,' which
they had 'built for Pharaoh,' E.i.11 — doubtless, therefore, a
well-built city, not a mere collection of mud-hovels. And so
the story, in E.ii.5, of the daughter of Pharaoh going down to
bathe in the Nile, in the immediate proximity of the place
where Moses was born, implies that his parents, at all events,
lived not far from the royal residence. But, if the Israelites
lived in such a city together with the Egyptians, it must have
been even larger than London, and the difficulty of communication would have been thereby greatly increased. For we cannot suppose that the humble dwellings of these despised slaves
were in closest contiguity with the mansions of their masters.
And, in fact, several of the miracles, especially that of the 'thick
darkness,' imply that the abodes of the Hebrews were wholly apart
from those of the Egyptians, however difficult it may be to conceive how, under such circumstances, each woman could have
borrowed from her that 'sojourned in her house.' Thus we
should have now to imagine the time that would be required for
the poorer half of London going hurriedly to borrow from the
richer half, in addition to their other anxieties in starting upon
such a sudden and momentous expedition.

70. The story, however, will not allow us to suppose that they
were living in any such city at all. Having so large flocks and
herds, 'even very much cattle,' E.xii.38, many of them must have
lived scattered over the large extent of grazing ground, required
under their circumstances; and, accordingly, they are represented
as still living in 'the land of Goshen,' E. ix. 26. But how large

must have been the extent of this land? We can form some
judgment on this point by considering the number of lambs,
which (according to the story) must have been killed for the
Passover. The command was, 'They shall take to them every
man a lamb, according to the house of their fathers, a lamb for
an house: and, if the household be too little for the lamb, let
him and his neighbour, next unto his house, take it according
to the number of the souls; every man, according to his eating,
shall make your count for the lamb,' E.xii.3,4. JOSEPHUS
(de Bell. Jud. vi.9.3) reckons ten persons on an average for
each lamb; but, he says, 'many of us are twenty in a company.'
KURTZ allows fifteen or twenty. Taking ten as the average
number, two millions of people would require about 200,000
lambs; taking twenty, they would require 100,000. Let us
take the mean of these, and suppose that they required 150,000.
And these were to be all 'male lambs of the first year,' E.xii.5.
We may assume that there were as many female lambs of the
first year, making 300,000 lambs of the first year altogether.

71. But these were not all. For, if the 150,000 lambs
that were killed for the Passover comprised all the males of
that year, there would have been no rams left of that year
for the increase of the flock. And, as the same thing would
take place in each successive year, there would never be any
rams or wethers, but ewe-sheep innumerable. Instead, then,
of 150,000, we may suppose 200,000 male lambs of the first
year, and 200,000 female lambs, making 400,000 lambs of the
first year altogether. Now a sheepmaster, experienced in
Australia and Natal, informs me that the total number of sheep,
in an average flock of all ages, will be about five times that of
the increase in one season of lambing. So that 400,000 lambs
of the first year implies a flock of 2,000,000 sheep and lambs of
all ages. Taking, then, into account the fact, that they had also
large herds, 'even very much cattle,' we may fairly reckon that
the Hebrews, though so much oppressed, must have possessed at

this time, according to the story, more than two millions of sheep and oxen.

72. What extent of land, then, would all these have required for pasturage? Having made enquiries on the subject from experienced sheepmasters, I have received the following replies. One informs me that in *New Zealand* there are a few spots, where sheep can be kept *two* to the acre; in other places, *one* can be kept per acre; but, generally, two acres are obliged to be allowed for one sheep. Another writes as follows: —

In *Australia*, some sheep-runs are estimated to carry *one* sheep to an acre, and these, I think, are of the best quality. Others are estimated at different numbers of acres to a sheep, until as many as *six* acres are allowed for one sheep by the Government, for the purposes of assessment. If these lands were enclosed in small farms or paddocks, they would keep a much larger number. But, when shepherded in flocks, much grass is destroyed and trampled under foot, that, if the animal were kept in a state of comparative rest, would be available for its support. *Natal* is able to support a much greater number, principally from its climate, as well as from the fact that the proportion of good land is incomparably greater with reference to the extent of poor land. The small number of sheep kept here at present would afford no example, upon which an opinion could be formed. But I think that I am within the mark, when I say that *three* sheep will hereafter be found to be supported by an acre of land.

Let us allow *five* sheep to an acre. Then the sheep alone of the Israelites would have required 400,000 acres of grazing land, — an extent of country considerably larger than the whole county of Hertfordshire or Bedfordshire, and more than twice the size of Middlesex, — besides that which would have been required for the oxen.

73. We must, then, abandon altogether the idea of the people living together in one city, and must suppose a great body of them to have been scattered about in towns and villages, throughout the whole land of Goshen, in a district of 400,000 acres, that is, twenty-five miles square, larger than Hertfordshire (391,141 acres). But then the difficulty of informing such a population would be enormously increased, as well as that of their borrowing, when summoned in the dead of night, E.xii.29-36, to

the extent implied in the story. For, even if we supposed the
first message, to prepare, kill, and eat the Paschal lamb, communicated to the whole people within the twelve hours, and
acted on, when they were abroad in full daylight,—or that they
actually had had a previous notice, to 'take' the lambs on the
tenth day, and 'keep' them to the fourteenth,—yet how could
the *second* notice, to start, have been so suddenly and completely circulated? Not one was 'to go out at the door of
his house until the morning,' E.xii.22. Consequently, they
could not have known anything of what had happened in
Pharaoh's house and city, as also among his people throughout
the whole 'land of Egypt,' E.xii.29, until the summons from
Moses, or, at least, the news of the event, reached each individual house. The whole population of Hertfordshire, by
the census of 1851, was considerably under 200,000 (167,298).
We are to imagine then its towns and villages increased more
than *tenfold* in size or in number. And then we are to
believe that every single household, throughout the entire
county, was warned in twelve hours to keep the Feast of the
Passover, was taught *how* to keep it, and actually *did* keep
it; and that, further, they were warned again at midnight,
to start at once in hurried flight for the wilderness, when each
family was shut up closely in its own house, and strictly forbidden to come out of it till summoned, and they could not,
therefore, communicate the tidings freely, as by day, from one
person to a number of others.

CHAPTER XL. •

THE MARCH OUT OF EGYPT.

. 74. *And the children of Israel journeyed from Rameses to Succoth, about six hundred thousand on foot that were men, besides children. And a mixed multitude went up also with them, and flocks and herds, even very much cattle.* Ex.ii.37,38.

It appears from N.i.3, ii.32, that these six hundred thousand were the men in the prime of life, 'from twenty years old and upward, all that were able to go forth to war in Israel.' And, (as we have seen), this large number of able-bodied warriors implies a total population of, at least, two millions. Here, then, we have this vast body of people of all ages, summoned to start, according to the story, at a moment's notice, and actually started, not one being left behind, together with all their multitudinous flocks and herds, which must (73) have been spread out over a district as large as a good-sized English county. Remembering, as I do, the confusion in my own small household of thirty or forty persons, when once we were obliged to fly at dead of night,—having been roused from our beds with a false alarm, that an invading Zulu force had entered the colony, had evaded the English troops sent to meet them, and was making its way direct for our Station, killing right and left as it came along,— I do not hesitate to declare this statement to be utterly incredible and impossible. Were an English village of (say) two thousand people to be called suddenly to set out in this way, with old people, young children, and infants, what indescribable distress there would be! But what shall be said of a thousand

times as many? And what of the sick and infirm, or the women
in recent or imminent childbirth, in a population like that of
LONDON, where the births * are 264 a day, or *about one every
five minutes?*

75. But this is but a very small part of the difficulty. We
are required to believe that, in one single day, the order to
start was communicated suddenly, at midnight, to every single
family of every town and village, throughout a tract of country
as large as Hertfordshire, but ten times as thickly peopled;
—that, in obedience to such order, having first 'borrowed' very
largely from their Egyptian neighbours in all directions, (though,
if we are to suppose Egyptians occupying the *same* territory
with the Hebrews, the extent of it must be very much increased,) they then came in from all parts of the land of Goshen
to Rameses, bringing with them the sick and infirm, the young
and the aged ;—further, that, since receiving the summons, they
had sent out to gather in all their flocks and herds, spread over
so wide a district, and had driven them also to Rameses ;—and,
lastly, that having done all this, since they were roused at midnight, they were started again from Rameses that very same
day, and marched on to Succoth, not leaving a single sick or
infirm person, a single woman in childbirth, or even a 'single
hoof,' E.xii.26, behind them !

76. This is, undoubtedly, what the story in the book of Exodus
requires us to believe. E.xii.31–41,51. KURTZ, however, is
aware of some of the impossibilities involved in this statement,
and makes an effort in this manner to explain them away,
i.p.357–359.

'Just fancy two millions of people, with large herds of cattle, and all the
baggage of emigrants, with their wives, and children, and old men, obliged to
start in the most hurried way! What confusion, what difficulties, would in-

* The births in LONDON, for a week taken at random (*Times*, Sept. 3, 1862), were
1,852, and the deaths, 1,147.

evitably impede them during the first days of their journey! An ordinary caravan may travel fifteen or twenty miles a day. But such a procession could hardly be able to do half of this. Let it be remembered too that *fresh parties were constantly joining them*; and that this must have caused some disturbance and delay. We cannot imagine it possible that two millions of Israelites, whose residences were scattered over the whole land of Goshen, should all have met together at Rameses, many of them merely to retrace their steps. Moreover, if we consider that they were ordered to eat the Passover at the early part of the night in their own houses, and not to leave their houses until the morning, we shall see that it must have been actually *impossible* for them all to meet in Rameses the next morning, many of them from the most distant parts of Goshen.'

Ans. Yet the text before us says plainly, 'The children of Israel journeyed *from Rameses to Succoth*, about six hundred thousand on foot.'

'Rameses was the capital of the province. There, no doubt, Moses and Aaron were residing. The procession started thence; and, after the main body had set out, smaller parties came from all directions, as speedily as possible, and joined it at the point of the road nearest to their own dwellings. It is true that its site is not precisely known. But it is certain that it must have stood somewhere in the immediate neighbourhood of the king's palace. Now, whether we suppose the palace to have been in Heliopolis, Bubastis, or Zoan, (and we have certainly only these points to choose from,) the shortest road to the sea, taking into account the circuitous route, by which the Israelites went, Exiv.2, would be so long, that it would be necessary to travel seventeen or twenty miles a day, in order to accomplish the whole in three days. Others may believe it, if they please. But I cannot believe that such a procession, as we have described, could keep up a journey of seventeen or twenty miles a day for three days running. Even if they only *travelled* three days, it would certainly be necessary to assume, as THACKERDOOR does, that there were periods of rest of longer duration, that is, actual days of rest between the three marching days.'

Ans. But nothing whatever is said or implied about these 'days of rest' in the Scripture. There would surely have been some reference made to them, if they really occurred.

77. And now let us see them on the march itself. If we imagine the *people* to have travelled through the open desert, in a wide body, fifty men abreast, as some suppose (60) to have been the practice in the Hebrew armies, then, allowing an interval of a yard between each rank, the able-bodied warriors alone would have filled up the road for about *seven miles*, and the whole multitude would have formed a dense column more than *twenty-two miles long*,—so that the last of

the body could not have been started till the front had advanced
that distance, more than two days' journey for such a mixed
company as this.

And the sheep and cattle—these must have formed another
vast column, but obviously covering a much greater tract of
ground in proportion to their number, as they would not march,
of course, in compact order. Hence the drove must have been
lengthened out for many long miles. And such grass as there
was, if not eaten down by the first ranks, must have been trodden under foot at once and destroyed, by those that followed
them mile after mile. What then did those two millions of
sheep and oxen live upon during this journey from Rameses to
Succoth, and from Succoth to Etham, and from Etham to the
Red Sea?

78. Even if we supposed with KURTZ, contrary to the plain
meaning of the Scripture, that they did not all rendezvous at
Rameses, but fell into the line farther on, on the first day or
the second, still this would not in reality in any way relieve the
difficulty, of so many miles of people marching with so many
miles of sheep and oxen. It would only throw it on to a farther
stage of the journey. For when, on the third day, they turned
aside and 'encamped by the Sea,' E.xiv.2, what then did this
enormous multitude of cattle feed upon? KITTO, *Hist. of the
Jews*, p.177, says,—

The journey to this point had been for the most part over a desert, the surface
of which is composed of hard gravel, often strewed with pebbles.

What, again, did they eat the next day, when they crossed
the Sea? What on the next three days, when they marched
through the wilderness of Shur, and 'found no water,' E.xv.22?
Of this last stage of their march KITTO says, *ib.p.*191 :—

Their road lay over a desert region, sandy, gravelly, and stony, alternately. In
about nine miles they entered a boundless desert plain, called *El Ati*, white and
painfully glaring to the eye. Proceeding beyond this, the ground became hilly,
with sand-hills near the coast.

CHAPTER XII.

79. *And the children of Israel did eat manna for forty years, until they came to a land inhabited; they did eat manna until they came unto the borders of the land of Canaan.* E.xvi.35.

The *people*, we are told, were supplied with manna. But there was no miraculous provision of food for the herds and flocks. They were left to gather sustenance, as they could, in that inhospitable wilderness. We will now go on to consider the possibility of such a multitude of cattle finding any means of support, for forty years, under these circumstances.

80. And, first, it is certain that the story represents them as *possessing* these flocks and herds during the whole of the forty years which they spent in the wilderness. Thus, in the *second* year, Moses asks, 'Shall the flocks and the herds be slain for them to suffice them?' N.xi.22. And in the *fortieth* year we read, 'The children of Reuben and the children of Gad had a very great multitude of cattle,' N.xxxii.1. This, it is true, is said immediately after the capture of a great number of cattle and sheep from the Midianites, N.xxxi. But the spoil in that case was divided among all the people. And, therefore, if the tribes of Reuben and Gad could still be distinguished among the rest, as having a great multitude of cattle, they must have been so noted before the plunder of the Midianites. Accordingly, we find that, at the end of the *first* year, they kept the second Passover under Sinai, N.ix.5, and, therefore, we may

presume, had at that time, as before, 200,000 male lambs of the
first year (69) at their command, and two millions of sheep and
oxen close at hand.

81. Again, it cannot be supposed, as some have suggested, that
the flocks and herds were scattered far and wide, during the
sojourn of the people in the wilderness, and so were able the
more easily to find pasture. The story says nothing, and implies
nothing, whatever of this; but, as far as it proves anything, it
proves the contrary, since we find the whole body of people
together, on all occasions specified in the history. If, indeed,
they had been so dispersed, they would surely have required to
be guarded, by large bodies of armed men, from the attacks of
the Amalekites, Midianites, and others.

But, even if this was the case during the thirty-seven years,
about which the story is silent altogether, yet, at all events,
during nearly twelve months, — 'a year all but ten days,'
says KURTZ, — they were all collected under Sinai, while the
Tabernacle was in process of building, at the end of which time
the second Passover was kept. We must, therefore, conclude
that they came to Sinai with those immense bodies of sheep
and oxen, with which, three months before, they had set out
from Egypt. Hence we find the command in E.xxxiv.3,
'Neither let the flocks nor herds feed before that mount.'

82. Lastly, it cannot be pretended that the state of the country, through which they travelled, has undergone any material
change from that time to this. It is described as being then what
it is now, a 'desert land,' a 'waste howling wilderness,' D.xxxii.10.
'Why have ye brought up the Congregation of Jehovah into
this wilderness, that we and our cattle should die there? And
wherefore have ye made us to come up out of Egypt, to bring
us unto this evil place? It is no place of seed, or of figs, or of
vines, or of pomegranates; *neither is there any water to drink*,'
N.xx.4,5. From this passage it appears also that the water from
the rock did *not* follow them, as some have supposed. 'Beware

that thou forget not Jehovah, thy God, who led thee through
that great and terrible wilderness, wherein were fiery serpents,
and scorpions, and drought, *where there was no water.'* D.viii.
15. 'Neither said they, Where is Jehovah, that brought us up
out of the land of Egypt, that led us through the wilderness,
through a land of deserts and of pits, through a land of drought
and of the shadow of death, through a land that no man passed
through, and where no man dwelt?' Jer.ii.6.

83. Let us now see what Canon STANLEY tells us, first, as to
the nature of the country, through which the host of Israel
must have marched from the Red Sea to Sinai. (*Sinai and
Palestine.*)

The wind drove us to shore—the shore of Arabia and Asia. We landed in a
driving sand-storm, and reached this place, Ayun-Musa, the wells of Moses. It is
a strange spot, this plot of tamarisks, with its seventeen wells, *literally an island
in the desert*, and now used as the Richmond of Suez, a comparison which chiefly
serves to show what a place Suez itself must be. Behind that African range lay
Egypt, with all its wonders,—the green fields of the Nile, the immense cities, the
greatest monuments of human power and wisdom. *On this Asiatic side begins immediately a wide circle of level desert, stone, and sand*, free as air, but with no trace
of human habitation or art, where they might wander, as far as they saw, for ever
and ever. And, between the two, rolled the deep waters of the Red Sea, rising and
falling with the tides, which, except on its shores, none of them could have seen,—
the tides of the great Indian Ocean, unlike the still dead waters of the Mediterra-
nean Sea.

The day after leaving Ayun-Musa was at first within sight of the blue channel
of the Red Sea. But soon Red Sea and all were lost in a sandstorm, which lasted
the whole day. (I have retained this account of the sand-storm, chiefly because it
seems to be a phenomenon peculiar to this special region. VAN EGMONT, NIE-
BUHR, Miss MARTINEAU, all noticed it; and it was just as violent at the passage
of a friend in 1841, and again of another two months after ourselves in 1853.)
Imagine all distant objects entirely lost to view,—the sheets of sand floating along
the surface of the desert, like streams of water, the whole air filled with a tempest
of sand, driving in your face like sleet.

We were, undoubtedly, on the track of the Israelites; and we saw the spring,
which most travellers believe to be Marah, and the two valleys, one of which must
almost certainly, both perhaps, be Elim. The general scenery is either immense
plains, [*i.e. bare and barren plains of sand*, as described below,] or, latterly, a succession of watercourses, [*without water*, see below,] exactly like the dry bed of a

F 2

Spanish river. These gullies gradually bring you into the heart of strange black and white mountains. *For the most part the desert was absolutely bare.* But the two rivals for Elim are fringed with trees and shrubs, *the first vegetation we have met in the desert.* First, there are the wild palms, successors of the 'three-score and ten,' not like those of Egypt or of pictures, but either dwarf, that is, trunkless, or else with savage, hairy trunks, and branches all dishevelled. Then there are the feathery tamarisks, here assuming gnarled boughs and hoary heads, on whose leaves is found what the Arabs call manna. Thirdly, there is the wild acacia, but this is also tangled by its desert growth into a thicket,—the tree of the Burning Bush and the Shittim-wood of the Tabernacle. . . A stair of rock brought us into a glorious wady, enclosed between red granite mountains, descending precipitously upon the sands. I cannot too often repeat that these wadys are exactly like rivers, *except in having no water*; and it is this appearance of torrent-bed and banks, and clefts in the rocks for tributary streams, and at times even rushes and shrubs fringing their course, which *gives to the whole wilderness a doubly dry and thirsty aspect,—signs of 'Water, water, everywhere, and not a drop to drink.'*

Here too began the curious sight of the mountains, streaked from head to foot, as if with boiling streams of dark red matter poured over them,—really the igneous fluid spurted upwards, as they were heaved from the ground. The road lay through what seemed to be the ruins, the cinders, of mountains calcined to ashes, like the heaps of a gigantic foundry. p.96-71.

There are at first sight many appearances, which, to an unpractised eye, seem indications of volcanic agency. But they are all, it is believed, illusory. The vast heaps, as of calcined mountains, are only the detritus of iron in the sandstone formation. The traces of igneous action in the granite rocks belong to their first up-heaving, not to any subsequent convulsions. Everywhere there are signs of the action of water, nowhere of fire. p.22.

84. Such then is the track, along which, according to the story, the two millions of Israelites had to pass with their two millions of sheep and oxen. Let us now see what Canon STANLEY tells us about the state of vegetation generally in the Sinaitic peninsula.

Another feature [of the mountains of this peninsula] is the infinite complication of jagged peaks and varied ridges. This is the characteristic described by Sir F. HENNIKER, with a slight exaggeration of expression, when he says that the view from Jebel Musa is 'as if Arabia Petræa were an ocean of lava, which, while its waves were running mountains high, had suddenly stood still.' It is an equally striking and more accurate expression of the same, when he speaks of the whole range as being the 'Alps unclothed.' This—*their union of grandeur with desolation*—is the point of their scenery absolutely unrivalled. They are the Alps of Arabia, but the Alps planted in the desert, and, therefore, stripped of all the clothing, which goes to make up our notions of Swiss or English mountains,—stripped of the variegated drapery of oak, and birch, and pine, and fir, of moss, and grass, and fern, which to landscapes of European hills are almost as essential as the rocks and peaks themselves. The very name of Alp is strictly applied only to the green pasture-lands, enclosed by rocks or glaciers,—a sight in the European Alps so common, in these Arabian Alps so wholly unknown. *p.13.*

The general character of the wadys, as well as of the mountains, of Sinai is *entire desolation.* If the mountains are naked Alps, the valleys are dry rivers, p.16. For a few weeks or days in the winter, these wadys present, it is said, the appearance of rushing streams. But their usual aspect is absolutely bare and waste, only presenting the image of thirsty desolation the more strikingly, from the constant indications of water, which is no longer there. *p.15.*

There is nearly everywhere a *thin,* it might almost be said, a *transparent,* coating of vegetation. There are occasional spots of verdure, which escape notice in a general view, but for that very reason are the more remarkable, when observed. Not, perhaps, every single tree, but every group of trees, lives in the traveller's recollection, as distinctly as the towns and spires of civilised countries. . . . The more definitely marked spots of verdure, however, are the accompaniments, not of the empty beds of winter torrents, but of the few living, perhaps perennial, springs, which, by the mere fact of their rarity, assume an importance difficult to be understood in the moist scenery of the West and North. The springs, whose sources are for the most part high up in the mountain clefts, occasionally send down into the wadys rills of water, which, however scanty, however little deserving of the name even of brooks, yet become immediately the nucleus of whatever vegetation the desert produces. (RUPPELL notices *four* perennial brooks.) Often their course can be traced, not by visible water, but by a tract of moss here, a fringe of rushes there, a solitary palm, a group of acacias, which at once denote that an unseen life is at work. *p.15–16.*

The highest of these [peaks of Mount Serbal] is a huge block of granite. On this you stand, and overlook the whole peninsula of Sinai. Every feature of the extraordinary conformation lies before you, — the wadys, coursing and winding in every direction, —the long crescent of the Wady es Sheikh, — the infinite number of mountains like a model, their colours all clearly displayed, the dark granite, the brown sandstone, the yellow desert, the dots of vegetation along the Wady Feiran, and the one green spot of the great palm-grove (if so it be) of Rephidim. *p.72*

85. We thus see the character of this desert, in which this immense number of cattle was sustained, according to the story, for the space of forty years. Canon STANLEY will not, however, evade the difficult question, which is thus raised ; and this is his comment upon it, *p.23–27,* with the replies which must be made to the different parts of his argument.

(i) 'The question is asked, How could a tribe, so numerous and powerful, as on any (?) hypothesis the Israelites must have been, be maintained in this inhospitable desert? It is no answer to say that they were maintained by miracles. For, except the manna, the quails, and the three interventions with regard to water, none such are mentioned in the Mosaic history; and, if we have no warrant to take away, we have no warrant to add.'

Ans. But, even if the people were supported by miracles, yet there is no provision whatever made in the Scripture for the support of the cattle. And these would need water as well as green food; and from N.xx.6, D.viii.15, it appears that the miraculous supply of water was not permanent. And so Kalisch observes, Exod.p.227 — 'The great scarcity of water in the Peninsula of Sinai is universally known.' 'In a space of 316 miles,' says Harmer, 'over part of this wilderness, Mr. Irwin found only four springs of water. In another space of 115 miles, he found only four springs, at one of which the water was brackish, and at another unwholesome.'

We shall presently produce the testimony of other writers on this point.

(ii) 'Nor is it any answer to say that this difficulty is a proof of the impossibility, and, therefore, of the unhistorical character, of the narrative. For, as Ewald has well shown, the general truth of the wanderings in the wilderness is an essential preliminary to the whole of the subsequent history of Israel.'

Ans. Ewald certainly asserts this; but I cannot find any place where he shows it. The story of the Exodus is, no doubt, an 'essential preliminary' to certain parts of the subsequent history of Israel, as recorded, but not to the whole of it. If that story be shown to be untrue, those parts may also have to be abandoned as untrue, but not the whole Jewish history.

(iii) 'Much may be allowed for the spread of the tribes of Israel far and wide through the whole peninsula, and also for the constant means of support from their own flocks and herds.'

Ans. I doubt if any allowance can be made for such spreading (81). The Mosaic narrative says nothing of any such a dispersion of the people. And, surely, the whole tone of it implies that they were kept constantly together, under the direct personal control of Moses. As before observed, if the cattle had been scattered in the way here supposed, they would have needed to be guarded by large bodies of armed men, from the attacks of other hostile tribes. But the numbers of the warriors of each tribe are carefully summed up in N.i.ii; and the position of each camp is assigned in N.ii, with distinct directions how they were to march, in front, and in the rear, and on either side of the Levites bearing the Tabernacle. And the names of all the marches thus made are recorded in N.xxxiii.

Besides which, it seems to be clearly implied in N.ix.17-23 that they travelled all together, and were not separated into different bodies, as Stanley supposes. 'When the cloud was taken up from the Tabernacle, then after that the children of Israel journeyed; and in the place, where the cloud abode, there the children of Israel pitched their tents.' 'Whether it were two days, or a month, or a year, that the cloud tarried upon the Tabernacle, remaining thereon, the children of Israel

abode in their tents, and journeyed not; but, when it was taken up, they journeyed.'
Who, in these verses, are meant by 'the children of Israel'? Surely, the same
who, a few verses before, in the same chapter, are ordered to keep the second Passover in the wilderness of Sinai, N.ix.1,2,—that is, the whole body of the people.
It appears to me a plain evasion of the distinct meaning of the Scripture, only resorted to in order to escape from a position of extreme difficulty, to suggest, as
Kurtz does, ill.p.306, that such words as the above are to be understood only of
Moses and Aaron and the Tabernacle, guarded, perhaps, by a troop of armed men,
going about in circuit continually to visit the different scattered knots of families.

But, at all events, they were all, according to the story, assembled together
under Mount Sinai, in one of the most desolate parts of the whole peninsula; and
they continued there for nearly twelve months, and had their flocks there, since at
the end of that time they kept the second Passover, N.ix.5.

Doubtless, they may be supposed to have derived some support from the
slaughter of their flocks and herds. The question is, how were the flocks and herds
themselves supported?

(iv) 'Something, too, might be elicited from the undoubted fact, that a population nearly, if not quite, equal to the whole permanent population of the peninsula,
does actually pass through the desert, in the caravan of the five thousand African
pilgrims on their way to Mecca.'

Ans. But the population, which we are now considering, was *two millions,* not
five thousand.

And these two millions of all ages had been driven out of Egypt in haste, and
'had not prepared for themselves any victual,' and had no means of carrying food,
if they had had it. Whereas the Mecca caravan will, no doubt, have made all due
preparation for the journey long beforehand, and will carry with it, we must
suppose, ample store of provisions on the backs of its camels.

Again, the two millions remain twelve months at a time in one most desolate
spot, and wander forty years in the dry and weary land. Whereas the caravan
merely passes through in a few days at the most.

Lastly, the Israelites had, according to the story, vast multitudes of cattle, which
had to be sustained in the desert without miraculous help. But the caravan has no
flocks or herds, and travels with camels, which can go for weeks without water.

(v) 'But, among these considerations, it is important to observe what indications
there may be of the mountains of Sinai having ever been able to furnish greater re-
sources than at present. These indications are well summed up by RITTER.'

Ans. Whatever they may be, they cannot do away with the plain language of
the Bible already quoted, which shows that the general character of the desert was
as desolate and barren then as now.

(vi) 'There is no doubt that the vegetation of the wadys has considerably decreased.
In part, this would be an inevitable effect of the violence of the winter-torrents.
The trunks of palm-trees washed up on the shore of the Dead Sea, from which the
living tree has now for many centuries disappeared, show what may have been

the devastation produced among these mountains, where the floods, especially in earlier times, must have been violent to a degree unknown in Palestine; whilst the peculiar cause, the impregnation of salt, which has preserved the vestiges of the older vegetation *there*, has *here*, of course, no existence. The traces of such destruction were pointed out to BURCKHARDT on the eastern side of Mount Sinai, as having occurred within half a century before his visit; also to WELLSTED, as having occurred near Tur in 1832.'

Ans. That palm-trees are found, washed up on the shores of the Dead Sea, into which they found their way, no doubt, from the river Jordan, gives surely no shadow of ground for believing that such trees, or any other, grew in the wilderness of Sinai. STANLEY himself writes of the Dead Sea, *p.293*,—

'Strewn along its desolate margin, lie the most striking memorials of this last conflict of life and death,— trunks and branches of trees, torn down from the thickets of the river-jungle, by the violence of the Jordan, thrust out into the sea, and thrown up again by its waves.'

It does not appear *why* the floods are supposed to have been more violent in earlier times than now. But, supposing that they were, and much more violent than in Palestine, and that BURCKHARDT and WELLSTED saw the traces of the devastation caused by them, it is notorious that the flood of one year, by the deposit which it leaves, rather *assists* than otherwise the vegetation of the next year. A few trees may be washed away; but the *general verdure*, which concerns most the present question of the *cattle*, would be promoted by a heavy fall of rain.

(vii) 'In fact, the same result has followed from the reckless waste of the Bedouin tribes— reckless in destroying, and careless in replenishing. A fire, a pipe, lit under a grove of desert trees, may clear away the vegetation of a whole valley. . . Again, it is mentioned by RUPPELL, that the acacia trees have been of late years ruthlessly destroyed by the Bedouins for the sake of charcoal; especially since they have been compelled by the Pasha of Egypt to pay a tribute in charcoal, for an amount committed on the Mecca caravan in the year 1823. Charcoal is, in fact, the chief — perhaps, it might be said, the *only* — traffic of the peninsula. Camels are constantly met, loaded with this wood on the way between Cairo and Suez. And, as this probably has been carried on to a great degree by the monks of the convent, it may account for the fact, that, whereas in the valleys of the eastern clusters this tree abounds more or less, yet in the central cluster itself, to which modern tradition certainly, and geographical considerations probably, point as the mountain of the 'burning thorn,' and the scene of the building of the Ark and all the utensils of the Tabernacle, *from this very wood*, there is now not a single acacia to be seen.' Compare STANLEY's statement from ocular observation, with the bold assertion of HÄVERNICK, *Pent.p.264.* 'The most important material, the wood for the Tabernacle, is just that which is found here most plentifully.'

Ans. It is possible that the *Ark* may have been made of the wood of this acacia (*Notal mimosa*), of which the Hebrews may have found a few trees in the desert. But it is certainly a very noticeable fact, that 'not a single acacia' is now to be seen in the very region, where, according to the story, not merely the Ark, with the vessels of the Tabernacle, but the Tabernacle itself, was built, with its forty-eight boards of shittim (acacia) wood, each 10 cubits by 1½ cubit, that is, 18½ ft. long by 2½ ft. broad, Ex.xxvi.20–30. It may be doubted if the 'probable' labours of the monks, in burning charcoal during late years, are enough to account for such a complete disappearance of the tree. In Natal, trees of this kind are cut down for firewood; and, by wasteful or excessive cutting, a piece of good bush-land may be stripped of all the trees, which are fit for such a purpose. But there will still remain a multitude of young trees and small saplings, which have sprung up from the seed shed by the old ones, and have not been cut down, because utterly useless as firewood.

Besides, the destruction of trees would not affect directly the growth of grass, on which the flocks and herds depended in the case of the Israelites, however (as STANLEY suggests in the next passage) it might, perhaps, affect it indirectly, but surely to a very slight and almost inappreciable degree, by diminishing the quantity of moisture attracted to the land.

(viii) 'If this be so, the greater abundance of vegetation would, as is well known, have furnished a greater abundance of water; and this again would react on the vegetation, from which the means of subsistence would be procured.'

Ans. The general answer to the above is, that the Bible speaks of the desert in exactly the same terms as those, which would even now be used to describe it. Especially, the extreme scarcity of water is expressly noticed. It is plain, therefore, that the removal of a few acacias has not materially changed the face and character of the country.

(ix) 'How much may be done by a careful use of such water and such soil as the desert supplies, may be seen by the only two spots, to which, now, a diligent and provident attention is paid, namely the gardens at the Wells of Moses, under the care of the French and English agents from Suez, and the gardens in the valleys of Jebel Musa, under the care of the Greek monks of the convent of St. Catherine. Even so late as the seventeenth century, if we may trust the expression of MONCONYS, the Wady-er-Rahah, in front of the convent, now entirely bare, was a vast green plain,' *une grande champagne verte.*

And so writes SHAW, *Travels to the Holy Land,* ch.ii : —

'Though nothing that can be properly called soil is to be found in these parts of *Arabia,* these monks have, in a *long process of time* (N.B.), covered over, with dung and the sweepings of their convent, near four acres of these naked rocks, which produce as good cabbages, salads, roots, and all kinds of pot-herbs, as any soil and climate whatsoever. They have likewise raised apple, pear, plum, almond, and olive trees, not only in great numbers, but also of excellent kinds. Their grasses also are not inferior, either in size or flavour, to any whatsoever. Thus this little garden demonstrates how far an indefatigable industry may prevail over nature.'

Ans. But the fact, that, in a few favoured spots, by great care and industry, and *in a long process of time,* 'little gardens' like this have been raised, is no proof that in the peninsula generally, for forty years, and in particular at the foot of

Sinai, for twelve months together, *at a moment's notice*, such an immense body of cattle could have been provided with the food and water they required. The expression of Moncunys, 'if we may trust it,' may have reference to the 'thin transparent coating of vegetation,' of which Stanley himself speaks (84). But, whatever it may mean, the desert was then, as it is now, a 'great and terrible wilderness,' a 'land of drought and of the shadow of death.'

(x) 'And that there was, in ancient times, a greater population than at present, — which would again, by thus furnishing heads and hands to consider and to cultivate these spots of vegetation, tend to increase and preserve them, — may be inferred from several indications.

'The Amalekites, who contested the passage of the desert with Israel, were — if we may draw an inference from this very fact, as well as from their wide-spread name and power, even to the time of Saul and David, and from the allusion to them in Balaam's prophecy, as 'the first of the nations,' — something more than a mere handful of Bedouins.'

Ans. If the Pentateuch be mainly unhistorical, we can take no account of the power of the Amalekites, as described in it. In the story of Saul's dealing with them, 1S.xv, and David's, 1S.xxx, there is nothing to show that they were any other than a powerful Arab tribe, between which and Israel there was a deadly feud.

Besides, did the Amalekites live *in* the desert of Sinai? On the contrary, we have the express statement of the Prophet, that it was 'a land that no man passed through, and where no man dwelt,' Jer.ii.6.

(xi) 'The Egyptian copper-mines, and monuments, and hieroglyphics, in Surabit-el-Khadim and the Wady Maghareh, imply a degree of intercourse between Egypt and the peninsula in the earliest days of Egypt, of which all other traces have long ceased.'

Ans. This does not help to prove in any way that two millions of people, with their two millions of sheep and oxen, could have lived under Sinai for twelve months, and could have been maintained for forty years in a country, which was then described as 'a desert land, a waste howling wilderness.' Supplies of corn were, no doubt, forwarded regularly by the king of Egypt for his workmen; and they had no vast flocks and herds that we know of.

(xii) 'The ruined city of Edom, in the mountains east of the Arabah, and the remains and history of Petra itself, indicate a traffic and a population in these remote regions, which now seem to us almost inconceivable.'

Ans. But Stanley himself writes, *p.87* : —

'The first thing that struck me, in turning out of the Arabah, up the defiles that lead to Petra, was that we had suddenly *left the desert*. Instead of the absolute nakedness of the Sinaitic valleys, we found ourselves walking on grass, sprinkled with flowers, and the level platforms on each side were filled with sprouting corn. And this continues through the whole descent to Petra, and in Petra itself.'

He elsewhere describes Petra, p 94, as 'an oasis of vegetation in the desert hills.' There was a reason, therefore, for Petra maintaining a certain amount of population in former days, as it might do now, which does not exist for the valleys of Sinai. But, even then, Petra had no population to support like that of Israel, and no such multitudinous flocks and herds.

(xiii) 'And even much later times, extending to the sixth and seventh centuries of our era, exhibit signs both of movements and habitations, which have long ago ceased, such as the writings of Christian pilgrims on the rocks, whether in the Sinaitic character, in Greek, or in Arabic, as well as the numerous remains of cells, gardens, chapels, and churches, now deserted and ruined, both in the neighbourhood of Jebel Musa and Serbal.'

Ans. But the fact of a few thousand pilgrims paying a passing visit to such places, bringing, probably, supplies of food with them, or of a number of monks and hermits contriving to live in the neighbourhood of one or two favoured spots, avails little to show how Israel could have lived under Sinai itself for so many months together, with such immense flocks and herds, or how they could have marched to and fro in the peninsula, from station to station, journeying ' by day or by night, when the cloud was taken up,' and abiding in their tents, ' whether it were two days, or a month, or a year,' when the cloud rested, N.ix.18-23, but finding all along the necessary supplies of food, and wood, and water, for themselves and their cattle. The pilgrims and hermits needed only to find their own scanty fare: they had no flocks and herds as the Israelites.

Canon STANLEY adds in conclusion,—' It must be confessed that none of these changes solve the difficulty, though they may mitigate its force. But they, at least, help to meet it : and they must under any circumstances be borne in mind, to modify the image, which we form to ourselves, of what must have always been — as it is even thus early described to be—'a great and terrible wilderness.' '

I have the more closely examined and carefully weighed the above arguments, because we may be certain that, by so able and earnest an advocate, every thing has been said, that well could be said, to make it in any way credible, that the means of support could have been found for so large a body of cattle in the peninsula of Sinai, without a special miracle, of which the Bible says nothing. The reader will be able to judge for himself to what these arguments really amount, even when most fully and favourably stated.

86. Before passing on, it may be well to quote also, and consider, the remarks of KALISCH on this point, *Exod.p.*212,213 :—

'The following circumstances may serve to obviate the objections:—

(i) 'During by far the greater part of the period of forty years (thirty-six years), the Israelites lived near the populous Mount Seir and the Red Sea, where they could not fail to come into commercial intercourse with rich nations and tribes, which provided them easily (?)—[a population as large as that of London!]—with all the necessaries of life.'

Ans. The Scripture-story says not a word about this long sojourn near Mount Seir and the Red Sea; at least, all it says is contained in D.ii.1: 'Then we turned and took our journey into the wilderness by the way of the Red Sea, as Jehovah spake unto me; and we compassed Mount Seir many days.' And, certainly, the notion of the Israelites 'having commercial intercourse with rich nations and tribes,' during almost all the time of their sojourn in the 'waste, howling wilderness,' the 'land that none passed through, and where no man dwelt,' is utterly opposed to the ordinary view. But, supposing that we admit the above, we should still have to account for the subsistence of the flocks and herds during the rest of the forty years, and particularly during the first three months, and during the twelve months passed under Sinai.

(ii) 'Nearly a whole year the Israelites encamped in the fertile (?) region around the Sinai, where the air is pure and refreshing, where fountains abound (?), and a variety of game is found (!), see N.xi.31, [where we find an account of the *miracle* of the gift of quails!].'

Ans. We reply to the above by referring to Stanley's description, quoted above (84) of the valleys, as well as the mountains, of Sinai, whose 'general character is entire desolation,' whose 'usual aspect is absolutely bare and waste, only presenting the image of thirsty desolation the more strikingly, from the constant indications of water, which is no longer there.' But, supposing that we granted this also, we should still have to account for the cattle surviving the march *to* and *from* Sinai.

(iii) 'Even the nomadic Bedouins are still now in the habit of cultivating the districts which appear suitable for agriculture; they live during this time in tents, and change their abode after every harvest. Thus several tribes may be met with even now, which are at the same time nomads and agriculturists; and nothing forbids us to suppose the same practice among the Israelites, during their sojourn in the desert, especially as some parts of the peninsula are extremely inviting to agriculture.'

Ans. To any ordinary reader the story forbids the supposition that the people were scattered away from the Sanctuary, in different parties, all over the peninsula. Not a word is said or implied of such dispersion in the Scripture; and during the whole time, which the Scripture does describe, they lived in one body together, except, of course, when a force was detached for a time for purposes of war, as the 12,000, who were sent for the conquest of Midian, N.xxxi. It is, therefore, a mere arbitrary assumption, opposed to all the indications which are given us in the narrative.

But spots of verdure, which might be cultivated by a few hundreds of Arabs, would not suffice for the wants of two millions of people. And, even if they did, we have still, as before, to explain how the *sheep and oxen* lived on in the dreary waste.

(iv) 'The Israelites brought numerous herds and flocks with them from Egypt, which furnished them with clothes and food of various kinds. It is natural to assume that they did not neglect the breeding of cattle on their journeys; and even the Biblical narrative leads us to suppose that especially the three tribes of Reuben, Gad, and Manasseh remained faithful to their former occupations, and, as proprietors of large flocks and herds, requested Moses to allot them, as their inheritance, the rich districts east of the Jordan, with their fertile pastures.'

Ans. But this involves the main difficulty itself, viz. how were these 'large flocks and herds' sustained in the wilderness?

(v) 'The Israelites had no want of gold and silver, and other precious property, to buy from the commercial caravans which traversed the desert, or from the neighbouring nations, many necessaries, especially corn,—a fact which is clearly alluded to in D.ii.6.'

Ans. But they could not at all events have bought *grass*, or other food, for their flocks and herds. Even D.ii.6 speaks only of their buying from the Edomites, when they reached the neighbourhood of Mount Seir. As to their march generally during the forty years, it is described as a march 'through the wilderness, through a land of deserts and pits, through a land of drought and of the shadow of death, through a land that no man *passed through*,'—they met with no *caravans*, therefore,—'and where no man *dwelt*,' Jer.ii.6.

(vi) 'It is universally acknowledged that Arabia Petræa was formerly considerably richer, and could maintain many more souls, than is the case in its present neglected state. Various circumstances may contribute to the deterioration of a country; and Arabia Petræa is not the only district in which such unfavourable change has taken place.'

Ans. But the Bible speaks of the district as having been then, in the time of the Exodus, a 'great and terrible wilderness, a land of drought and of the shadow of death.'

(vii) 'The tribes may either singly, or in a united body, have made excursions from Kadesh for the purpose of procuring provisions.'

Ans. Then they must have found their way out of the wilderness: it is hardly to be believed that they would have returned again to wander about in the waste. But, at all events, they could hardly have brought back with them, from such excursions, sufficient supplies of fodder to support their two millions of live stock.

(viii) 'It is well-known that the inhabitants of these climates require comparatively but little food for their subsistence and the support of their physical strength.'

Ans. Is the same true of the sheep and oxen of these climates? Or rather, can they live on year after year, altogether *without* any supplies of grass and water?

(ix) 'It sufficed perfectly, if the Israelites were but scantily provided with the most necessary wants. Abundance or superfluity would have led them away from their great aim, the conquest of Canaan, especially after so long wanderings; whilst the scarcity of their subsistence kept their longing, after their better and permanent abodes, uninterruptedly alive.'

Ans. Still the difficulty remains about the flocks and herds.

(x) 'Lastly, if all these natural circumstances combined should not be deemed sufficient to account for the sojourn of the Israelites in the desert during forty years, the holy text informs us of the constant supply of manna, a nutritious and agreeable food, with which they were abundantly furnished during that whole period.'

Ans. But the *sheep and oxen* could not live upon the manna, nor could the people *drink* it; and N.xx.6, D.viii.15, show that the water from the rock did not follow them throughout the desert.

Upon the whole it will be plain that HALLECK adds but little to the number, and nothing whatever to the force, of STANLEY's arguments. Indeed, he himself admits, *Exod.p.*211, in direct opposition to his *fourth* argument above, —

'After the people had wandered a whole month through barren districts, the stores, which they might have brought with them from Egypt, must have been exhausted, *especially as, no doubt, a great part of their cattle had perished on the march* (from the Red Sea) *from thirst and want of proper food.'*

67. But it may be well now to quote one or two passages from other writers, which yet more plainly develope the absolute barrenness of this wild and desolate region, as it now appears, and as, we have every ground from the Bible itself to believe, it must *then* have appeared also.

In *winter*, when the whole of the upper Sinai is *deeply covered with snow*, and many of the passes are choked up, the mountains of Moses and Saint Catherine are often inaccessible. Mr. FAZAKERLY, who ascended them in the month of February, found a great deal of snow, and the ascent was severe. 'It is difficult,' he says, ' to imagine a scene more desolate and terrific, than that which is discovered from the summit of Sinai. A haze limited the prospect, and, except a glimpse of the sea in one direction, nothing was within sight but snow, huge peaks, and crags of naked granite.' Of the view from Mount Saint Catherine he says, 'The view from hence is of the same kind, only much more extensive than from the top of Sinai. It commands the two gulfs of Akaba and Suez; the island of Tiran and the village of Tur were pointed out to us; Sinai was far below us; all the rest, wherever the rye could reach, was a vast wilderness, and c confusion of granite mountains and valleys destitute of verdure.' COXDEX's *Modern Traveller*, Arabia, p.159,160.

88. We have here another question raised, which is not generally taken into consideration at all. The Israelites, according to the story, were under Sinai for nearly twelve months together, and they kept the second Passover under the mountain before they left it, N.ix.1. As this was in the first month of the Jewish ecclesiastical year, corresponding to the latter part of March and beginning of April, they must have passed the whole of the winter months under Sinai, and must have *found it bitterly cold.*

In the mountainous districts it is very cold in the winter nights. Sometimes the water in the garden of the monastery at Saint Catherine freezes even in February. And, on the contrary, in the summer months, the sun pours down his rays burning hot from heaven, and in reflection from the naked rocky precipices, into the sandy valleys. BURRELL, quoted in HANNEMANN's *Palann*, Clark's Theol. Library, p.838.

Where, then, amidst the scanty vegetation of the neighbourhood, where at the present time there seems not to grow a single tree fit for firewood,— and there is no reason to suppose that it was ever otherwise,—did the Israelites obtain supplies of fuel, not only for the daily cooking necessities of a population like that of LONDON, but also for relief against the piercing cold of the winter season, or when, as JOSEPHUS says, *Ant.*iii.7.4, ' the weather was inclined to snow?' And the cattle,—unless supplied with artificial food, must they not also have perished in multitudes from cold and starvation under such circumstances? We find this to be the case even in the fertile colony of Natal, where in some winter seasons they die from these joint causes in great numbers, when the grass, though abundant, is dried up, and the cold happens to be more severe than usual, though not severe enough for ice and snow, except in the higher districts, and then only for about a month or six weeks in the year.

89. If the last quotations describe the state of things in the

depth of *winter*, the following, (in addition to the words of
RÜPPELL, above quoted,) will convey some idea of the general
aspect of the country in the height of the *summer* season. It
would seem that travellers generally choose the *most favourable
season of the year* for visiting these desert regions. We must
make due allowance for this fact also, in considering even their
accounts of the desolate barrenness of the whole district, with
reference to the story told in the Pentateuch.

BURCKHARDT visited Um Shaumer, the loftiest mountain in the peninsula, and
writes of the scene as follows. 'The devastations of torrents are everywhere
visible, the sides of the mountains being rent by them in numberless directions.
The surface of the sharp rocks is blackened by the sun; all vegetation is dry and
withered; and the whole scene presents nothing but utter desolation and hopeless
barrenness.' CONDER's *Arabia*, p.199.

He afterwards travelled from the neighbourhood of Sinai eastward, across the
peninsula, to the gulf of Akaba. But, he says, 'the barrenness of this district
exceeded anything we had yet witnessed, *except some parts of the desert of El Tih*
[that is, the desert of Sinai]. The Nubian valleys might be called pleasure-grounds
in comparison. Not the smallest green leaf could be discovered. And the thorny
mimosa, which retains its verdure in the tropical deserts of Nubia with very little
supplies of moisture, was here entirely withered, and so dry that it caught fire from
the lighted sabre which fell from our pipes as we passed.' *Ibid.*p.204.

90. As to the little spots of greater luxuriance, which are
found here and there in the Sinaitic peninsula, we may form
some idea of their character, and of the fitness of any one of
them to sustain even for a single day such a vast multitude of
cattle, from the following description by BURCKHARDT of Wady
Kyd, 'one of the most noted date-valleys of the Sinai Arabs.'
This valley he entered, and pursued its windings, till he came in
an hour's time to a small rivulet, two feet across and six inches
in depth, *which is lost immediately below in the sands of the
Wady.*

It drips down a granite rock, which blocks up the valley, there only twenty
paces broad, and forms at the foot of the rock a small pond, overshadowed by
trees, with fine verdure on its banks. The rocks, which overhang it on both sides,
almost meet, and give to the whole the appearance of a grotto, most delightful to
the traveller, after passing through these dreary valleys. It is, in fact, the most
romantic spot I have seen in these mountains. The source of the rivulet is half an

hour higher up the valley, the deep verdure of which forms a striking contrast with the glaring rocks, showing that, wherever water passes in these districts, vegetation invariably accompanies it. Beyond the spot, where the rivulet comes out of the ground, *vegetation ceases*, and the valley widens. Notwithstanding its verdure, however, Wady Hyd is an uncomfortable halting-place, on account of the great number of gnats and ticks, with which it is infested. *Ibid.p.318.*

Bearing in mind that two millions of sheep and oxen, allowing a space of three feet by two feet as *standing* ground for each, would require, when packed together as closely as in a pen in a cattle-market, nearly 300 acres of land, it seems idle to expend more time in discussing the question, whether they could have been supported in the wilderness by the help of such insignificant wadies as these, which a drove of a hundred oxen would have trampled down into mud in an hour.

CHAPTER XIII.

01. *I will send my fear before thee, and will destroy all the
people to whom thou shalt come, and I will make all thine
enemies turn their backs unto thee. And I will send hornets
before thee, which shall drive out the Hivite, the Canaanite, and
the Hittite, from before thee. I will not drive them out from
before thee in one year, lest the land become desolate, and the
beast of the field multiply against thee. By little and little I
will drive them out from before thee, until thou be increased
and inherit the land.* E.xxiii.27–30.

The whole land, which was divided among the tribes in the
time of Joshua, including the countries beyond the Jordan, was
in extent about 11,000 square miles, or 7,000,000 acres.
(KITTO's *Geogr. of the Holy Land, Knight's series, p.7.*) And,
according to the story, this was occupied by more than two
millions of people. Now the following is the extent of the
three English agricultural counties of Norfolk, Suffolk, and
Essex, with the population according to the census of 1851: —

	Acres.	Pop. in 1851.
Norfolk contains	1,354,301	442,714
Suffolk	947,681	337,215
Essex	1,060,649	369,318
	3,362,531	1,149,247

By doubling the above results, we find that these counties of
England are, at this very time, about as thickly peopled as the

land of Canaan would have been with its population of Israelites only, without reckoning the aboriginal Canaanites, who already filled the land, — 'seven nations, *greater* and *mightier'* than Israel itself, D.iv.38, vii.1, ix.1, xi.23. And surely it cannot be said that these three Eastern Counties, with their flourishing towns of Norwich, Lynn, Yarmouth, Aylsham, Cromer, Thetford, Wisbench, Bungay, Beccles, Lowestoff, Ipswich, Southwold, Bury St. Edmunds, Sudbury, Woodbridge, Harwich, Colchester, Chelmsford, Romford, Malden, &c., and their innumerable villages, are in any danger of lying 'desolate,' with the beasts of the field multiplying against the human inhabitants.

92. But, perhaps, a still better comparison may be instituted with a country, which resembles in many respects, in its natural features and other circumstances, the state of Canaan in those early days. The colony of Natal has an extent of 18,000 square miles, and a population, white and black included, probably not exceeding 150,000 altogether. This population is, of course, very scanty, and the land will allow of a much larger one. Yet the human inhabitants are perfectly well able to maintain their ground against the beasts of the field. And, in fact, the lions, elephants, rhinoceroses, and hippopotami, which once abounded in the country, have long ago disappeared. Leopards, wild boars, hyænas, and jackals are killed occasionally in the bush. But many a white man may have lived for years in the colony, as I have done, and travelled about in all parts of it, without seeing or hearing one. But the population of the land of Canaan, (2,000,000 inhabitants within less than 12,000 square miles,) would have been more than *twenty times as thick* as that of Natal, (150,000 within 18,000, or 100,000 within 12,000 square miles). Natal, in fact, should have a population of 3,000,000 instead of 150,000, in order to be compared for density of population with the land of Canaan, according to the story, after the entrance of the Israelites, without reckoning the old inhabitants.

CHAPTER XIV.

03. *All the first-born males, from a month old and upwards, of those that were numbered, were twenty and two
thousand two hundred and threescore and thirteen.* N.iii.43.

Let us see what this statement implies, when treated as a
simple matter of fact. For this purpose I quote the words of
KURTZ, iii.p.200 : —

If there were 600,000 males of twenty years and upwards, the whole number of
males may be reckoned at 900,000, [he elsewhere reckons 1,000,000,] in which case
there would be only one first-born to *forty-two* [forty-four] males. In other words,
the number of boys in every family must have been on the average *forty-two*.

This will be seen at once if we consider that the rest of the
900,000 males were *not* first-borns, and, therefore, each of these
must have had one or other of the 22,273 as the first-born of
his own family, — except, of course, any cases where the first-
born of any family was a *daughter*, or was *dead*, of which we
shall speak presently.

And these were not the first-born on the *father's* side, as
MICHAELIS supposes, so that a man might have many wives and
many children, but only one first-born, as was the case with
Jacob himself. They are expressly stated to have been the first-
born on the *mother's* side — 'all the first-born that openeth the
matrix,' N.iii.12. So that, according to the story in the Pentateuch, *every mother of Israel must have had on the average
forty-two sons!*

94. How then is this difficulty to be explained? Kurtz says : —

'We must enquire whether there are no other means — (than that suggested by Michaelis, which the Scripture will not allow, as Kurtz admits,—) of explaining the fact, that, on an average, there was only one first-born to forty-two males.'

And Kurtz is bold enough to say, 'There are plenty;' and proceeds to state them as follows.

(i) 'The first is the rarity of polygamy, which lessened the proportion of the first-born.'

Ans. Kurtz means to say that, if polygamy had prevailed among them, the difficulty would have been enormously increased, and, as he says himself, 'rendered perfectly colossal.' For, in that case, if a man had had four wives, and had had children by each of them, he must have had on the average forty-two sons by each. So, then, the rarity of polygamy, (which, indeed, Kurtz assumes without proof,) does not at all help to *lessen* the difficulty already existing in the incredible statement, that every mother in Israel had, on the average, forty-two male children.

(ii) 'A second is the large number of children to whom the Israelitish mothers gave birth.'

Ans. This, again, is assumed without proof, or, rather, directly in the face of all the facts which are given us, by which to judge of the size of the Hebrew families. We have no reason whatever to suppose, from the data which we find in the Pentateuch, that the mothers of Israel were prolific in any unusual degree. We read of one, two, three, &c. sons, just as in ordinary families, occasionally of six or seven, once of ten, G.xlvi.21, but not of an *average of ten*, or fifteen, or twenty. The average in G.xlvi is *five* sons, and in E.vi it is *three*. And, as regards *daughters*, all the indications are *against* their being as numerous even as the sons. Jacob had only one daughter, G.xlvi.15; Asher had only *one*, G.xlvi.17; Amram had only *one*, N.xxvi.59; Zelophehad had *five*, but no sons, N.xxvi.33.

(iii) 'Thirdly, the constantly recurring expression, 'Every first-born that openeth the womb,' warrants the conclusion, that the first-born of the father was not reckoned, unless he was also the first-born of the mother.'

Ans. This would only apply to a very small number of cases, where a man had married a woman, who had borne children before he married her, and who had, therefore, been a widow or a harlot.

But, in point of fact, it does not affect the present question at all. The woman's first-born will still have been numbered, whoever the father was. And the result is, as before, that there are reckoned only 22,273 first-born sons of all the mothers of Israel, after one or other of whom the other males must all be ranged in their respective families, (except, as before, cases, where the first-born of a family was either a female or was dead,) so that each mother must have had on the average forty-two sons.

(iv) 'Fourthly, it leads also to the still more important assumption, that, if the first-born was a *daughter*, any son, that would be born afterwards, would not be reckoned at all among the first-borns. Now statistical tables show that the first-born is more frequently a female than a male.'

Ans. But in the case of the Hebrews, according to the story in the Pentateuch, (whatever may be the case generally,) the first-born was much more frequently a male than a female. We have the instances of Abraham, and Isaac, and Jacob, and Jacob's twelve sons, (except Asher who had a daughter before going into Egypt, and she may have been his first-born child,) in each of which the first-born was a male. Amram's first-born, indeed, was a daughter, and Zelophehad had only daughters. As far, however, as we have any data to guide us, we should be justified in assuming that the number of the first-born males far exceeded that of the females.

But let us suppose that they were even equal in number, — that, in short, besides the 22,273 first-born males, there were also 22,273 first-born females. This, however, will not by any means get rid of, or at all diminish, the essential difficulty of the question now before us : it will only change the form of it. For, having now brought in the idea of the *daughters*, we must remember that, if there were 900,000 [1,000,000] males, there must have been about as many females. And 44,546 first-born children among a population of 1,800,000, would imply that each mother had, on the average, forty-two children, as before, but twenty-one sons and twenty-one daughters.

(v) 'Lastly, such of the first-born, as were themselves heads of families, were not reckoned at all as first-born, who had to be redeemed, but only their sons.'

Ans. This is a pure assumption, and unwarranted by anything that is found in the Scripture. The command in N.iii.40 is, 'Number *all* the first-born of the males, from a month old and upward.' Hence, says Kurtz, very justly, 'if there had been any age, beyond which the numbering was not to go, [or, we may add, any class of persons, such as heads of families, who were to be excepted from it,] it would undoubtedly have been mentioned here. But there is nothing of the kind.'

Have we any reason to suppose that the first-born son of an Egyptian was exempt from death, because he was the head of a family ? He was the first-born to his father, and therefore died, according to the story in Exodus, 'from the first-born of Pharaoh that sat on his throne, unto the first-born of the captive that was in the dungeon,' so that 'there was not a house where there was not one dead.' E.xii.29,30.

Besides, it seems to be implied that the 22,273 first-borns were intended to include *all* the first-born males of all ages, whether married men and heads of families, or not, from the simple fact, that the 22,000 male Levites, of all ages and conditions, from a month old and upward,' whether heads of families or not, were substituted for 22,000 of the first-borns 'from a month old and upward,' the remaining 273 first-borns being redeemed with money, N.iii.39,45,46.

95. Thus not one of KURTZ's 'many ways' of relieving this difficulty is really of any use whatever for that purpose. There is, indeed, one point, though he has not noticed it, which might help slightly to diminish it. In some families the first-born may have died before the numbering; some, too, who were born about the time of the birth of Moses, may have been killed by the order of Pharaoh. And, if all those, who may have thus died, be reckoned with the 22,273, the proportion of the remaining males, to be placed under each of the first-born, will be somewhat altered. Still we cannot suppose any unusual mortality of this kind, without checking in the same degree the increase of the people. Let us, however, reckon that one out of four first-borns died, so that instead of 44,546 first-borns, male and female, there would have been, if all had lived, about 60,000. But even this number of first-borns, for a population of 1,800,000, would imply that each mother had on the average thirty children, fifteen sons and fifteen daughters. Besides which, the number of *mothers* must have been the same as that of the *first-borns*, male and female, including also any that had died. Hence there would have been only 60,000 child-bearing women to 600,000 men, so that only about one man in ten had a wife or children !

96. The following is the account which HÄVERNICK gives of this matter, *Pent.p.308.*

(i) 'The proper solution of this difficulty is that of J. D. MICHAELIS, that this statement supplies a proof that at that time *polygamy must have prevailed to an unusual extent amongst* the Israelites, and a like conclusion is supplied by the genealogies in Chronicles; comp. especially 1Ch.vii.4, 'for they had many wives and sons.' For, in that case, the proportion of the first-born to the other children is regulated by the Hebrew usage, that the first-born must be such on the father's as well as the mother's side; see G.xlix.3,4, N.i.20, D.xxi.15-17, Pa.cv.36.'

Ans. KURTZ, as we have seen (94), rejects this supposition of MICHAELIS, as inconsistent with the Scripture and wholly untenable. There is no reason to believe that polygamy *did* prevail at that time among the Hebrews; in 1Ch.vii.4 the polygamy in the case of the 'sons of Issachar' appears to belong to the time of David, v.2, and is spoken of rather as the exception than the rule. The 'Hebrew usage' has nothing to do with the present question. We are here only concerned with 'all the first-born, whatsoever *openeth the womb*,' E.xiii.2, 'bring males,' e. 15. What is the use of quoting such passages as G.xlix.3, 'Reuben, thou art my first-born,' N.i.20, 'Reuben, Israel's eldest son,' Ps.cv.36, 'He smote also all the first-born in the land,' or D.xxi.15–17, where the *son's* first-born is 'not to be disinherited upon private affection'?

(ii) 'That this also related to purchasing exemption from Priestly service, is clear from E.xxii.29, 'the first-born of thy sons shalt thou give unto me,' and E.xxxiv.20, 'All the first-born of thy sons thou shalt redeem,' where, of course, only one of the sons can be thought of as the *primogenitus.*'

Ans. There is no reason to suppose that in these passages only the first-born by one wife is intended, more especially as they must be explained by such words as those in E.xiii.12,13, 'Thou shalt set apart unto Jehovah all that *openeth the matrix* . . . the males shall be Jehovah's . . . and all the first-born of man among thy children shalt thou redeem.'

(iii) 'The meaning must also not be restricted by the phrase that is frequently subjoined, 'that openeth the matrix;' for this addition is to give prominence to primogeniture on the maternal side. This latter, however, alone could not make one the first-born of the family; for that, being the first-born on the father's side was also an essential requisite.'

Ans. If we were to suppose, contrary to the plain statements of the Bible, that only those were reckoned who were first-borns on the *father's* as well as the *mother's* side, yet even then, while the *impossibility* would be removed of each mother bearing forty-two children, there would remain the *improbability* of each *father* on the average having forty-two children, when there is not the slightest indication of any such fecundity in the story.

(iv) 'Accordingly, it is only from this passage that a conclusion can be drawn as to the historical condition of the people, which is confirmed also by notices elsewhere.'

I am wholly at a loss to understand the meaning of the above paragraph.

97. BUNSEN (*Bibl. Jahrb.* p.ccclxi-ccclxiv) admits the difficulty existing in the Scripture statement, of which, he says, 'no satisfactory explanation has ever yet been given.' His own mode of explanation is as follows: —

He considers that the command to dedicate the first-born males to Jehovah was intended to prevent among the Hebrews the practice of sacrificing them to Moloch, which he speaks of as common among the Syrian tribes. And he suggests, therefore, that the first-borns were numbered ' from a month old and upward' up to six or seven years only, which he supposes to be the age at which such children were sacrificed.

Ans. (i) Something would surely have been said about the age being limited to six or seven years, if that had been intended.

(ii) The expression, 'from a month old and upward,' which is used of the first-borns in N.iii.40,13, is used also in the very same chapter, r.15,22,28,34,39, of the whole body of male Levites, and certainly without any idea of such limitation. It is impossible to believe that the very same expression is employed in two successive verses, r.39,40, with such very different meanings attached to it, and without the least intimation of any such a difference.

98. The Rev. T. Scott has another way of explaining the difficulty : —

The first-born in any company must in general amount to at least one in eight or ten; whereas the number here mentioned was scarcely one in fifty of all the males, young and old ; for there were above 600,000 adults, and, perhaps, almost as many under age. It is, therefore, evident that none were numbered, but those who had been born after the destruction of the first-born of Egypt. This, indeed, seems to be the meaning of the law, which referred to the *future*, and not to the *past*, E.xiii.2 ; and it is evident that the firstlings of the cattle were thus reckoned. Indeed, 45,000 of both sexes, which is rather more than double the first-born males, seems a vast number of first-born children within the space of one year. But, upon reflection, we shall find it to be by no means improbable that among 1,200,000 persons of both sexes, who were above twenty years of age, (and many might marry much younger than that age,) there should be within that time 50,000 marriages,—that is, about the twelfth part of the company of marriageable persons of each sex. Especially, if we consider that multitudes might be inclined to marry, when they found that they were about to enjoy liberty: and when they recollected that the promises made to Israel peculiarly respected a very rapid increase, and that there would, doubtless, be a very great blessing upon them in this respect.

Ans. (i) The reason here assigned, for an extra number of marriages at the time of their leaving Egypt, is very far-fetched. Immediately before the last great plague, they had asked only to go a *three days' journey* into the wilderness, to sacrifice unto Jehovah, E.v.3, x.24–26 ; and *up to that time* they had had no assurance of immediate and permanent deliverance from their state of bondage.

(ii) *After that time* it is inconceivable that these extra marriages took place in the hurry and confusion of the *first three months*, (since the children, according to Scott, were now born, at the time of the numbering, *at the end of the first year*,) during that distressing march through the wilderness of Sin to Sinal.

(iii) It would be far more reasonable to say that, as they expected at that time to march directly into the Promised Land, any, that wished to be married, would be likely to put off their wedding-joys till a more convenient season, and, if the young people were eager for matrimony, their judicious parents would be likely to restrain their impetuosity.

(iv) If, therefore, these 45,000 first-borns of both sexes were born during the year after they left Egypt, we must consider that they were rather *under*, than *over*, the annual average.

(v) But these are *first-borns* only, and, according to Scott himself, the whole number of births must be *eight* or *ten* times as great, say 400,000, in order to maintain the proper proportion of the number of first-borns to that of the whole population. Whereas, in the city of London, the whole number of births in a week is about 1,662; and, therefore, in a year, only 96,801!

(vi) But what decides the question at once is, that there is not the slightest intimation given in the story, N.iii.40–43, that these first-borns were to be only those that were born after the death of the first-born in Egypt. On the contrary we are told, 'Moses numbered, as Jehovah commanded him, *all the first-born* among the children of Israel.'

99. By this time, surely, great doubt must have arisen, in the mind of most readers, as to the historical veracity of sundry portions of the Pentateuch. That doubt, I believe, will be confirmed into a certain conviction, by its appearing plainly from the data of the Pentateuch itself, that there could not have been any such population as this, to come out of Egypt, — in other words, that the children of Israel, at the time of the Exodus, could not, if only we attend carefully to the distinct statements of the narrative, have amounted to two millions,— that, in fact, the whole body of warriors could not have been *two thousand*.

In order, however, to show this more clearly, we must first premise a few considerations, which are set forth in the two following chapters.

CHAPTER XV.

100. *Now the sojourning of the children of Israel, who dwelt in Egypt, was four hundred and thirty years.* E.xii.40.

The question, which we have here to consider, is this,— To what 'sojourning' do the above words refer, — whether to that of Jacob and his descendants in the land of Egypt *only*, or to the entire sojourning of them and their forefathers, Abraham and Isaac, 'in a strange land,' both in Canaan and Egypt, from the time when the promise of old was given to Abraham, and he 'sojourned in the land of promise, as in a strange country,' Heb.xi.9 ?

The verse above quoted, as it stands in the E. V., does not decide the question.

But there is evidently something unusual and awkward in the manner, in which the phrase, 'who dwelt in Egypt,' enters into the above passage. And, in fact, the original words would be more naturally translated, (as in the Vulgate, Chald., Syr., and Arab. Versions,) 'the sojourning of the children of Israel, *which they sojourned in Egypt*,' but for the serious difficulties which would thus arise.

101. In the first place, St. Paul, referring to 'the covenant, that was confirmed before of God' unto Abraham, says, 'the Law, which was *four hundred and thirty years after*, cannot disannul it,' Gal.iii.17. It is plain, then, that St. Paul dates the beginning of the four hundred and thirty years, not

from the going down into Egypt, but from the time of the promise made to Abraham.

102. Again, in E.vi.16-20, we have given the genealogy of
Moses and Aaron, as follows:—

'There are the names of the Sons of Levi, according to their
generations, Gershon, and Kohath, and Merari. And *the years
of the life of Levi were a hundred thirty and seven years.*

'And the sons of Kohath, Amram, and Izhar, and Hebron,
and Uzziel. And *the years of the life of Kohath were a hundred
thirty and three years.*

'And Amram took him Jochebed, his father's sister, to wife;
and she bare him Aaron and Moses. And *the years of the life of
Amram were a hundred thirty and seven years.*'

Now supposing that Kohath was only an *infant*, when
brought down by his father to Egypt with Jacob, G.xlvi.11, and
that he begat Amram at the very end of his life, when 133
years old, and that Amram, in like manner, begat Moses, when
he was 137 years old, still these two numbers added to 80 years,
the age of Moses at the time of the Exodus, E.vii.7, would
only amount to 350 years, instead of 430.

103. Once more, it is stated in the above passage, that 'Amram
took him Jochebed, his father's sister,'— Kohath's sister, and
therefore, Levi's daughter,— to wife.' And so also we read,
N.xxvi.59. 'The name of Amram's wife was Jochebed, *the
daughter of Levi, whom (her mother) bare to him in Egypt.*'

Now Levi was one year older than Judah, and was, therefore, 43
years old (20), when he went down with Jacob into Egypt; and
we are told above that he was 137 years old, when he died.
Levi, therefore, must have lived, according to the story, 94
years in Egypt. Making here again the extreme supposition of
his begetting Jochebed in the last year of his life, she may have
been an infant 94 years after the migration of Jacob and his
sons into Egypt. Hence it follows that, if the sojourn in Egypt
was 430 years, Moses, who was 80 years old at the time of the

Exodus, must have been born 350 years after the migration into
Egypt, when his mother, even on the above extravagant supposition, must have been at the very least 256 years old.

104. It is plain, then, that the 430 years are meant, as St.
PAUL understood, to be reckoned from the time of the call
of Abraham, when he yet lived in the land of Haran. Thus,
reckoning 25 years from his leaving Haran, G.xii.4, to the birth
of Isaac, xxi.5, 60 years to the birth of Jacob, xxv.26, 130 years
to the migration into Egypt, xlvii.9, we have 215 years of sojourning *in the land of Canaan,* leaving just the same length of
time, 215 years, for the sojourn *in the land of Egypt.*

This will agree better with the statements made above as to
the birth of Moses, though even then not without a strain upon
one's faith. Thus Moses was born 80 years before the Exodus,
or 135 years after the migration into Egypt. And Levi may
have had Jochebed born to him, (as Abraham had Isaac,) when
100 years old, that is to say, 57 years after the migration
into Egypt, since he was at that time 43 years old (103); in
which case Jochebed would have been 78 years old when she
bare Moses, younger, therefore, by 12 years than Sarah at the
birth of Isaac, G.xvii.17.

105. We must conclude, then, that the translation in the English Bible of E.xii.40, however awkwardly it reads, is correct as
it stands, *if the Hebrew words themselves are correct,* as they
appear in all manuscript and printed copies of the Pentateuch.

The LXX, however, and the Samaritan Version, insert a few
words, which are either a gloss to make the meaning of the passage more plain, or else are a translation of words, which existed
in those copies of the Hebrew Bible, which were used for those
Versions, though not found in our own. The Vatican copy of the
LXX renders the passage thus : 'The sojourning of the children
of Israel, which they sojourned *in Egypt and in the land of
Canaan, was 430 years.*' The Alexandrian has, 'The sojourning
of the children of Israel, which *they and their fathers*

sojourned *in Egypt and in the land of Canaan*, was 430 years.'
The Samaritan has, 'The sojourning of the *children of Israel
and of their fathers*, which they sojourned *in the land of
Canaan and in the land of Egypt*, was 430 years.'

In fact, during all those 430 years, Abraham and his seed
were, according to the story, sojourning as strangers ' in the land
of promise as in a strange land,'—in a land which ' was not their
own,' but for the present ' the possession of the Gentiles.'

106. And this agrees also substantially with the promise in
G.xv.13-16, which is quoted by St. STEPHEN, Acts vii.6: 'Know
of a surety that thy seed shall be a stranger, in a land that is not
theirs, and shall serve them, and they shall afflict them, *four
hundred years*. And also that nation, whom they shall serve,
will I judge; and afterwards they shall come out with great substance. And thou shalt go to thy fathers in peace; thou shalt
be buried in a good old age. But *in the fourth generation*
they shall come hither again; for the iniquity of the Amorites is
not yet full.'

At first sight, indeed, it would seem from the above that
Abraham's descendants were to be *afflicted* for 400 years, in
one land, such as Egypt, by one nation. But it is certain that
they were *not* afflicted, according to the story, during *all* the
time of their sojourn in Egypt. And hence it appears that the
time here specified, 400 years, is meant to refer to the
time during which the ' Seed of Abraham ' should be *sojourners*
in a strange land, rather than to the oppression, which they
were to suffer during some part of that sojourning. They lived
as ' pilgrims and strangers ' in the land of Canaan; and they
were at times, no doubt, much more uncomfortable among the
people of that land, G.xxvi.15-21, xxxiv, than they were in
Egypt during the seventy years while Joseph yet lived (110),
and, we may suppose, for some time after his death.

107. We conclude, then, that the 400 years In the above passage are meant to date from the birth of Isaac, ' Abraham's seed,'

from which to the Exodus there may be reckoned, as in (104),
405, or, in round numbers, 400, years.   If, indeed, we suppose
that five years may be considered to have elapsed, after Abram
was called in Ur of the Chaldees, before he reached the land of
Canaan, during which interval God 'brought him out of Ur of
the Chaldees,' G.xv.7, and 'he came out of the land of the
Chaldeans, and dwelt in Charran, and from thence, after his
father's death, God removed him into the land of Canaan,'
Acts vii.4,— we shall have exactly 400 years from the birth of
Isaac to the Exodus, and the sojourn in Egypt will be 210,
instead of 215, years, by which the difficulties still existing (104),
with respect to the birth of Moses, will also be somewhat
relieved.   [See also the latter part of (110).]

CHAPTER XVI.

108. AGAIN, when it is said, G.xv.16, 'in the *fourth* generation they shall come hither again,' this can only mean 'in the fourth generation,' reckoning from the time when they should leave the land of Canaan, and go down into Egypt. Thus we find Moses and Aaron in the fourth generation from the time of the migration, viz. Jacob — Levi — Kohath — Amram — Aaron. Or, as Jacob was so aged, and Moses and Aaron also were advanced in life beyond the military age, we may reckon from those, as Levi, who went down into Egypt in the prime of life, and then the generation of Joshua, Eleazar, &c., in the prime of life, will be the fourth generation.

109. Accordingly, if we examine the different genealogies of remarkable men, which are given in various places of the Pentateuch, we shall find that, as a rule, the contemporaries of Moses and Aaron are descendants in the *third*, and those of Joshua and Eleazar in the *fourth* generation, from some one of the *sons*, or *adult grandsons*, of Jacob, who went down with him into Egypt. Thus we have : —

	1st Gen.	2nd Gen.	3rd Gen.	4th Gen.	5th Gen.	
Levi	. . Kohath	Amram	Moses	.	.	.	.	E.vi.16,18,20
Levi	. . Kohath	Amram	Aaron	.	.	.	.	E.vi.16,18,20
Levi	. . Kohath	Uziel	Mishael	.	.	.	.	L.x.4.
Levi	. . Kohath	Uziel	Elzaphan	.	.	.	.	L.x.4.
Levi	. . Kohath	Izhar	Korah	.	.	.	.	N.xvi.1.
Reuben	. Pallu	Eliab	Dathan	.	.	.	.	N.xxvi.7-9.
Reuben	. Pallu	Eliab	Abiram	.	.	.	.	N.xxvi.7-9.

	1st Gen.	2nd Gen.	3rd Gen.	4th Gen.	5th Gen.		
Zarah .	. Zabdi	Carmi	Achan	.	.	. .	Jo.vii.1.
Pharez .	. Hezron	Ram ·	Amminadab	Nahshon	.	.	Ruth iv.18,19.
Pharez .	. Hezron	Segub	Jair	.	.	. .	1Ch.ii.21,22.
Pharez .	. Hezron	Caleb	Hur	Uri	Bezaleel		1Ch.ii.18–20.

In the last instance, Bezaleel is in the *fifth* generation from Pharez. Perhaps, he was a young man, and was reckoned in the generation next to that of Joshua: and, in fact, JOSEPHUS, *Ant.* iii. 6.1, calls him the 'grandson of Miriam,' who is regarded by Jewish tradition as the wife of Hur. Thus he would have been a contemporary of *Phinehas*, the *grandson* of Aaron, — not of his son, Eleazar. Besides, Hezron, as well as his father, Pharez, was born, according to the story, in the land of Canaan; so that Bezaleel was actually still in the fourth generation from one who went down into Egypt.

110. Again, we are told that the children of Machir, the son of Manasseh, were brought up upon Joseph's knees, G.l.23. Hence, as Joseph was 39 years old, when Jacob came down to Egypt (20 note), and died at the age of 110, G.l.22, having lived, therefore, 71 years after that event, we may assume that Machir's son, Gilead, was born about 70 years after the migration, and we read of 'Zelophehad, the son of Hepher, the son of Gilead,' whose daughters came to Moses for land, and who died in the wilderness, N.xxvii.1–3.

In fact, if the sojourn in Egypt had lasted 430 years, instead of 210 or 215, then 360 years must have intervened between the birth of Gilead and the Exodus; and we should have to suppose that Gilead had a son, Hepher, when 180 years old, and Hepher also had a son, Zelophehad, when 180 years old, that so Zelophehad might even have been born at the time of the Exodus, and been able to have full-grown daughters, as the story implies, at the end of the forty years' wanderings.

111. The above include *all* the instances, which I have been able to find, where the genealogies are given in the Pentateuch itself.

But in 1Ch.vii.22-27 we have a remarkable exception to the above rule, where we find the genealogy of Joshua given as follows:—'Joshua, the son of Nun, the son of Elishama, the son of Ammihud, the son of Laadan, the son of Tahan, the son of Telah, the son of Rephah, the son of Beriah, the son of Ephraim,'—that is to say, Joshua is given in the *ninth* generation from Ephraim, or the *tenth* from Joseph.

Upon this I would first remark as follows.

(i) This is an exception to the rule, which prevails *universally* in the Pentateuch.

(ii) We are not here concerned with the books of Chronicles, (which, says Scott, 'it is generally agreed were compiled by Ezra,' rather, perhaps, by the same author who wrote the book of Ezra, but which were certainly composed long after the Captivity,) but with the narrative in the Pentateuch itself and book of Joshua, and must abide by the data which they furnish.

(iii) The book of Chronicles itself exhibits the rule of the Pentateuch in other cases, as in that of Moses and Aaron, vi.1-3, Korah, vi.37,38, Achan, ii.4,6,7, Nahshon, ii.9,10, Bezaleel. ii.18,20, Jair. ii.21,22.

It is strange, then, that in this single instance of Joshua there should be so remarkable a variation from the general rule.

112. Let us now, however, examine more closely this statement in the book of Chronicles.

Since Joseph 'saw Ephraim's children of the third generation,' G.l.23, Telah, one of these, may have been born about seventy years after the migration into Egypt (110).

We have no express statement of the age of Joshua at the time of the Exodus. But we may suppose it to have been about the same as that of Caleb, the son of Jephunneh, with whom he is so often coupled; and Caleb was forty years old, when sent to spy the land at the end of the first year after the Exodus. Jo.xiv.7. We may, therefore, adopt the estimate of Josephus, *Ant.*v.1,29, who reckons the age of Joshua as *forty-five* at the time of the Exodus. This will agree well with the fact, that, shortly after leaving Egypt, while still young enough to be the 'minister' or servant of Moses, E.xxiv.13, he was old enough also to command the host of Israel in the fight against Amalek. E.xvii.9,10.

Hence, since the Exodus took place 215 years at most after the migration into Egypt, there must have intervened between the birth of Telah and that of Joshua 215—70-45, that is, 100 years; so that, according to the Chronicler, there must have been *six* complete generations in 100 years, which is hardly credible.

Again, according to the chronicler, 'Elishama, the son of Ammihud,' was the grandfather of Joshua. But 'Elishama, the son of Ammihud,' was himself the captain of the host of Ephraim, N.ii.18, about a year after his *grandson*, Joshua, had commanded the whole Hebrew force which fought with Amalek, E.xvii.8-16, which also is hardly credible.

113. But, in truth, the account of Joshua's descent in 1Ch.vii. involves a palpable contradiction.

Thus, in v.24, we are told that Ephraim's *daughter* built two villages in the
land of Canaan. If we suppose this to mean that the *descendants* of Ephraim's
daughter, after the conquest in the time of Joshua, did this, yet in v.22,23, we
have this most astonishing fact stated, that Ephraim himself, after the slaughter
by the men of Gath of his descendants in the *seventh* generation, 'mourned many
days,' and then married again, and had a son, Beriah, who was the *ancestor of
Joshua*! This Beriah, however, is not named at all among the sons of Ephraim
in the list given in N.xxvi.35.

KITTO remarks upon this point, *Hist. of the Jews*, p.146:—

'It is impossible that Ephraim should have been then alive to mourn over the
seventh generation of his descendants. Read 'Zabad' for 'Ephraim,' and all
becomes intelligible.'

This is, of course, mere conjecture, and it does not by any means dispose of the
difficulty: for, by this correction, as a little consideration will show, Joshua will
be made a descendant in the *seventeenth* generation from Joseph, to associate with
Eleazar in the *fourth* generation from Levi.

KURTZ, § 33.9, suggests that the expression 'and his son,' when occurring
in a genealogy, should be distinguished from 'his son,' the former only indicating an
additional son of the father last spoken of, one (or more) of whose sons has been
named already; so that, in other words, the former phrase expresses a *brother* of
the person last mentioned, while the latter denotes his son. Thus, in 1Ch.vii.20,
the expression 'and the sons of Ephraim, Shuthelah, and Bered his son, and
Tahath *his* son, &c.,' means only that Bered, Tahath, &c., as *well as* Shuthelah,
were sons of Ephraim, and brothers of one another. This would make the men
whom 'Ephraim their father mourned,' to be his own sons, and would at once get
rid of this particular contradiction.

Any remark of this most able and impartial critic deserves full consideration.
In reply, therefore, to the above suggestion,—

(i) I point to 1Ch.iv.13, 'and his son Rephaiah,' compared with the parallel
passage, viii.37, 'his son, Rapha;'

(ii) According to KURTZ, the eight persons named, in vii.20,21, would *all* be
brothers, and among them are *two* Shuthelahs, and *two* Tahaths, which can hardly
have been the case in the same family of brethren.

(iii) Further, if KURTZ's view were true, those named in v.25,26, Beriah,
Rephah, Resheph, Telah, Tahan, would also be sons of Ephraim for a similar
reason, and Joshua would be only in the *sixth* generation from Ephraim. Joseph
would now have seen the birth of Ephraim's great-grandson *Ammihud*. G.123,
between whose birth and that of Joshua there would be an interval of 100 years
(110): and this is quite long enough to allow of the *three* generations, Ammihud,
Elishama, Nun, Joshua. The result thus arrived at would, therefore, perfectly
agree with our other data: but, for the reasons above given, we cannot assent to
KURTZ's suggestion.

Upon the whole it is plain that we are justified in dis-

missing the whole account in the book of Chronicles, about the
genealogy of Joshua, as most probably erroneous, and, at all
events, of no importance whatever, in opposition to so many
testimonies from the Pentateuch and from the Chronicles itself,
all tending to the same result.

114. We conclude, then, that it is an indisputable fact, that
the story, as told in the Pentateuch, intends it to be understood
— (I) that the children of Israel came out of Egypt about 215
years after they went down thither in the time of Jacob,
— (ii) that they came out in the *fourth* generation from the
adults in the prime of life, who went down with Jacob.

And it should be observed that *the second of these conclusions
does not in any way depend upon the correctness of the former.*

Upon this point JOSEPHUS writes, *Ant.*ii.9.1 : —

Four hundred years did they spend under these afflictions; for they strove one
against the other which should get the mastery, the Egyptians desiring to destroy
the Israelites by their labours, and the Israelites desiring to hold out to the end
under them.

But, of course, the last words of the above can only refer to the
last portion of their sojourn in *Egypt*, since they were not
struggling with the Egyptians till after Joseph's death, at all
events.   And so writes JOSEPHUS again, *Ant.*ii.15.2 : —

They left Egypt four hundred and thirty years after our forefather Abraham
came into Canaan, but two hundred and fifteen years only after Jacob removed
into Egypt.

And he writes of Moses, *Ant.*ii.9.6 : —

Abraham was his ancestor of the seventh generation.

And so he says of Joseph, *Against Apion*, i.33 : —

He died four generations before Moses, which four generations make almost 170
years.

And Archd. PRATT observes, *Science and Scripture, p.*78:—

It was to be in the *fourth* generation that his seed were to return to Canaan.
But 430, or even 400, years is very much longer than four generations, and therefore must include something besides the bondage in Egypt, viz. the sojourning in

Canaan. His prediction regarding the 'fourth generation' was literally fulfilled. Moses and Aaron were sons of Jochebed, who was the daughter of Levi, N.xxvi.59, a text which incidentally confirms the correctness of our general outline. Eleazar, the Priest, the son of Aaron, was, therefore, of the fourth generation from Jacob [? Levi]. He returned to Canaan and died there, his father, Aaron, and that generation, having died in the wilderness.

115. From this it can be shown, beyond a doubt, that it is quite impossible that there should have been such a number of the people of Israel in Egypt, at the time of the Exodus, as to have furnished 600,000 warriors in the prime of life, representing, at least, two millions of persons, of all ages and sexes,— that is to say, it is impossible, *if we will take the data to be derived from the Pentateuch itself.*

CHAPTER XVII.

116. In the first place, it must be observed, as already noted, that we nowhere read of any *very large families* among the children of Jacob or their descendants to the time of the Exodus. We may suppose, in order that we may have the population as large as possible, that very few died prematurely, and that those, who were born, almost all lived and multiplied. But we have no reason whatever, from the data furnished by the Sacred Books themselves, to assume that they had families materially larger than those of the present day. Thus we are told in G.xlvi that Reuben had 4 sons, Simeon 6, Levi 3, Judah 5, Issachar 4, Zebulun 3, Gad 7, Asher 4, Joseph 2, Benjamin 10, Dan 1, Naphtali 4. It is certainly strange that, among all the 69 children and grandchildren and great-grandchildren of Jacob, who went down with him into Egypt, there should be only *one* daughter mentioned, and *one* granddaughter. The very numbering of these two among the 'seventy souls' shows that the females 'out of the loins of Jacob' were not omitted *intentionally.*

117. Some, indeed, have suggested that these two only were inserted, because they were either notorious already, as Dinah, or may have become notorious in after days, as may possibly have been the case with Asher's daughter, Serah, *v.*17, though the Bible says nothing about it. But it is plain that this is only perverting the obvious meaning of the Scripture in G.xlvi. It is certain that the writer intends it to be understood that

these seventy were the *only* persons, and these two the *only* females, who had at that time been born in the family of Jacob. And, though the fact itself, of this wonderful preponderance of males, may seem very strange, and would be so indeed in actual history, it is only another indication of the unhistorical character of the whole account. For the present, however, we may admit it as *possible* in the nature of things, that there should have been, at first at all events, such a preponderance of males, and even *probable*, if the house of Israel was to increase with extraordinary rapidity.

118. The twelve sons of Jacob, then, as appears from the above, had between them 53 sons, that is, on the average 4½ each. Let us suppose that they increased in this way from generation to generation. Then in the *first* generation, that of *Kohath*, there would be 54 males, (according to the story, 53, or rather only 51, since Er and Onan died in the land of Canaan, *v.* 12, without issue,) — in the *second*, that of *Amram*, 243, — in the *third*, that of *Moses* and *Aaron*, 1,094, — and in the *fourth*, that of *Joshua* and *Eleazar*, 4,923; that is to say, instead of 600,000 warriors in the prime of life, there could not have been 5,000.

Further, if the numbers of *all* the males in the four generations be added together, (which supposes that they were all living at the time of the Exodus,) they would only amount to 6,311. If we even add to these the number of the *fifth* generation, 22,154, who would be mostly children, the sum-total of males of all generations could not, according to these data, have exceeded 28,465, instead of being 1,000,000.

119. But in the above we have tacitly assumed that each man had daughters as well as sons. There must have been females born in the family of Jacob as well as males; and the females must have been as numerous as the males, if we are to suppose that all the males had families as above. 'Jacob's sons' wives,' it is true, are spoken of in G.xlvi.26, as *not* being out of his loins.

But, with the story of Isaac's and Esau's and Jacob's marriages before us, we cannot suppose that the wives of the sons of Jacob generally were mere heathens. Judah, indeed, took a Canaanitish woman for his wife or concubine, G.xxxviii.2. But we must not infer that all the other brothers did likewise, since we find it noted, as a special fact, that Simeon had, besides his other five sons, 'Shaul, the son of a Canaanitish woman,' G.xlvi.10. Joseph, again, compelled by the peculiarity of his situation, married an Egyptian lady, whom Pharaoh gave him to wife, G.xli.45. The other brothers, we may suppose, obtained their wives, as their fathers, Isaac and Jacob, did before them, from their relations in Haran.

120. But, however this may have been, we must suppose that in Egypt,—at all events, in their later days, for a hundred years or more, from the time that their afflictions began,—such friends were not accessible. We must conclude, then, that they either took as wives generally Egyptian heathen women, or else intermarried with one another. The former alternative is precluded by the whole tone and tenor of the narrative. As the object of the king was to keep down their numbers, it is not to be supposed that he would allow them to take wives freely from among his own people, or that the women of Egypt, (at least, those of the generation of Amram, which gave birth to Moses, and after it,) would be willing, generally, to associate their lot with a people so abject and oppressed as the Hebrews. Besides, we are told expressly that, in childbirth, 'the *Hebrew* women were not as the *Egyptian* women,' E.i.19, by which it is plainly implied that the wives of the Hebrews were also Hebrews.

The narrative itself, therefore, requires us to suppose that the Hebrew families intermarried, and that girls, as well as boys, were born to them freely in Egypt, though not, it would seem (117), in the land of Canaan.

121. Yet we have no ground for supposing, from any data

which we find in the narrative, that the whole number of the
family was on that account increased. On the contrary,
Zelophehad had *five* daughters, but *no* sons, N.xxvii.1; Amram
had *two* sons and one daughter, N.xxvi.59; Moses had *two* sons
and *no* daughter, E.xviii.3,4; Aaron had *four* sons and *no*
daughter, N.xxvi.60; Izhar, Amram's brother, had *three* sons,
E.vi.21, Uzziel had *three* sons, E.vi.22, Korah had *three* sons,
E.vi.24, Eleazar had *one* son, E.vi.25. In the last four cases
we cannot say whether, or not, there were any daughters. But,
if we take all the families given in E.vi.14–25, together with
the two sons of Moses, we shall find that there are 13 persons,
who have between them 39 sons, which gives an average of 3 sons
each. This average is a fairer one to take for our purpose than
the former; because these persons lived at all different times in
the interval, between the migration into Egypt and the Exodus.
We may suppose, also, that the average of *children* is still as
large as before, or even larger, so that each man may have had
on the average six children, three sons and three daughters;
since the females appear to be omitted purposely in E.vi, (as
we see by the omission of Amram's daughter, Jochebed,) though
they could not have been omitted in G.xlvi, as we have seen
above.

122. Supposing now the 51 males (118) of the *first* generation
(Kohath's) to have had each on the average three sons, and so
on, we shall find the number of males in the *second* generation
(Amram's) 153, in the *third* (Aaron's) 459, and in the *fourth*
(Eleazar's) 1377,—instead of 600,000.

In fact, in order that the 51 males of Kohath's generation
might produce 600,000 fighting men in Joshua's, we must suppose that each man had 46 children (23 of each sex), and each
of these 23 sons had 46 children, and so on!—of which prolific
increase, it need hardly be said, there is not the slightest indication in the Bible, except, indeed, in the statement of the
number of the first-borns, which has been already considered.

123. Bishop Patrick suggests, note on E.i.7, that the Hebrew women might, by 'extraordinary blessing of God,' have brought forth 'six children at a time'! It is plain that he felt very strongly the difficulty raised by the Scripture statement, and did not consider how this fecundity would affect the Hebrew *women*, as regards either the *birth*, or the *rearing*, of the children.

To the same effect writes Kalisch, *Exod.p.2* : —

We easily concur in the opinion that the Hebrew women gave birth to more than one child at a time, (Ebyn-Ezra, *twins*, Rasyi, *six* children). That this was not uncommon in Egypt we learn from Aristotle, *Hist.Anim.* vii.4: 'Often the women bring forth *twins*, as in Egypt. They even give birth to *three* or *four* children at a time; nor is this of rare occurrence. But *five* is the highest number, and there have been instances of such fruitfulness.' Pliny, *Nat. Hist.* vii.3, observes 'That *three* are born at a birth, is undoubted: to bear above that number is considered as an extraordinary phenomenon, except in Egypt.'

But the Scripture implies no such fecundity among the Hebrews, either in G.xlvi, or in E.vi, or in E.i.19, where the midwives say of the Hebrew women, ' they are delivered *ere the midwives come in unto them*,'— which could hardly have been said, if three or four children were often born at a time.

124. In 1Ch.ii.34,35, we read that Sheshan, a descendant of Judah in the ninth generation, 'had a servant, an *Egyptian*, whose name was Jarha ; and Sheshan gave his daughter to Jarha his servant to wife, and she bare him Attai,' whose descendants are then traced down through twelve generations, and are reckoned, apparently, as Israelites of the tribe of Judah. From this it would seem that Hebrew girls might be married to foreigners,— we may suppose, proselytes,— and their children would then be reckoned as ' children of Israel.' It is obvious that such cases would be comparatively rare. But let us suppose that each man had six children as in (121), three sons and three daughters, and that even *half* the daughters of Israel were married to foreign proselytes,— a most extravagant supposition. This would be equivalent to reckoning that each man had on the average — not 3 sons, but — 4½, as in (118). And the total number of warriors in the fourth generation, resulting from 51 progenitors, would, as before, not amount to 5,000.

CHAPTER XVIII.

125. WHEN, however, we go on further to examine into the details of this large number of male adults, the results will be found yet more extravagant.

Thus Dan in the first generation has *one* son, Hushim, G.xlvi. 23; and, that he had no more born to him in the land of Egypt, and, therefore, had *only* one son, appears from N. xxvi. 42, where the sons of Dan consist of only one family. Hence we may reckon that in the fourth generation he would have had 27 warriors descended from him, instead of 62,700, as they are numbered in N.ii.26, increased to 64,400 in N.xxvi.43.

In order to have had this number born to him, we must suppose that Dan's one son, and each of *his* sons and grandsons, must have had about 80 children of both sexes.

We may observe also that the offspring of the *one* son of Dan, 62,700, is represented as nearly double that of the *ten* sons of Benjamin, 35,400, N.ii.23.

126. Again we have in E.vi the genealogy, before quoted, of the three sons of Levi, who came with Jacob into Egypt,— Gershon, Kohath, Merari.

(i) These three increased in the *second* (Amram's) generation to 8, (not to 9, as it would have been, if they had had each three sons on the average,) viz. the sons of *Kohath* 4, of *Gershon* 2, of *Merari* 2, E.vi.17-19.

(ii) The 4 sons of *Kohath* increased in the *third* (Aaron's) generation to 8, (not to 12,) viz. the sons of Amram (Moses and Aaron) 2, of Izhar 3, of Uzziel 3, E.vi.20-22. If we now assume that the 2 sons of *Gershon* and the two sons of *Merari* increased in the same proportion, that is, to 4 and 4 respectively, then all the male Levites of the *third* generation would have been 16.

(iii) The two sons of Amram increased in the *fourth* (Eleazar's) generation to 6, viz. the sons of Aaron 4, (of whom, however, 2 died, N.iii.2,4,) and of Moses 2. Assuming that all the 16 of the third generation increased in the same proportion, then all the male Levites of the generation of Eleazar would have been 48, or rather 44, if we omit the 4 sons of Aaron who were reckoned as Priests. Thus the whole number of Levites who would be numbered at the first census would be only 44, viz. 20 *Kohathites*, 12 *Gershonites*, 12 *Merarites*, instead of 8,580, as they are numbered in N.iv.48, viz. 2,750 *Kohathites*, 2,630 *Gershonites*, and 3,200 *Merarites*, v.36,40,44.

127. Or we may put the matter in another, and a yet stronger, light, *using only the express data of Scripture*, and omitting all reference to the 215 years' sojourn in Egypt and to the four generations,—in fact, *making no assumptions of our own whatever.*

The Amramites, numbered as Levites in the fourth (Eleazar's) generation, were, as above, only two, viz. the two sons of Moses, the sons of Aaron being reckoned as Priests. Hence the rest of the Kohathites of this generation must have been made up of the descendants of Izhar and Uzziel, each of whom had *three* sons, E.vi.21,22. Consequently, since *all* the Kohathites of Eleazar's generation were numbered at 2,750, N.iv.36, it follows that these *six* men must have had between them, according to the Scripture story, 2,748 sons, and we must suppose about the same number of daughters!

128. There are some variations in the account given of the

Levite families in the book of Chronicles from that which we find in E.vi. We have already had reason to see (113) that the statements of the Chronicler are not always trustworthy. But it may be well to consider how far they would oblige us to modify the results we have just arrived at.

Thus, in E.vi, the sons of Libni and Shimi, v.17, are not mentioned. But in 1Ch.xxiii.8 we are told that the sons of Laadan (Libni) were three, v.8, and the sons of Shimei (Shimi) three, v.9, whose names are given as 'Shelomith, Haziel, and Haran, three.' In the very next verse, however, we read 'the sons of Shimei were Jahath, Zina, (or rather Zizah, v.11,) Jeush, and Beriah; these *four* were the sons of Shimei'; and it is obvious that their names are totally different from the three former names. It is added, v.11, 'And Jahath was the chief, and Zizah the second: but Jeush and Beriah had not many sons; therefore they were in one reckoning, according to their father's house.'

Again, in E.vi, while the sons of Amram, Izhar, and Uzziel are mentioned, no sons are assigned to their brother Hebron. In N.iii.27, however, we read of 'the family of the Hebronites'; and, in 1 Ch.xxiii.19 *four* sons of Hebron are mentioned.

So in E.vi.21,22, the sons of Izhar are *three*, and the sons of Uzziel, *three*: but in 1Ch.xxiii.18,20, Izhar has only *one* son, and Uzziel, *two*.

Collecting, however, the Chronicler's statements, we find that, in the *third* generation, the Gershonites were 7, viz. the sons of Laadan 3, of Shimei 4,—the Kohathites 9, viz. the sons of Amram 2, of Izhar 1, of Hebron 4, of Uzziel 2, — the Merarites 5, viz. the sons of Mahli 2, v.21, (but one of these had no sons, v.22,) of Mushi 3, v.23.

Thus, according to the Chronicler, all the male Levites in the *third* generation were 21, of whom one had no sons; whereas in (126) we have reckoned them as 16. It is plain, then, that the results in the *fourth* generation will not be materially different, if we take his data, from those which we have already arrived at.

129. The number of Levites at the second census, when compared with that at the first, involves also a great inconsistency. We are told, N.xxvi.62, that, at the *second* census, 'those that were numbered of them were 23,000, all males from a month old and upward.' And, at the *first* census, N.iii.39, 'All that were numbered of the Levites, all the males from a month old and upward, were 22,000.' Hence, during the thirty-eight years in the wilderness, they had only increased in number by 1,000 upon 22,000.

Now, either the Levites were included in the sentence passed
upon the Congregation generally, that they should die in the
wilderness, or they were not. The former supposition seems to
be precluded by the fact that Eleazar, the son of Aaron, at all
events, was alive, according to the story, even after the death of
Joshua, Jo.xxiv.33. And Eleazar was a full-grown Priest at
Sinai, E.xxviii.1, and was, therefore, we must suppose, above the
age of twenty, or even that of thirty, at which the Levites were
first allowed to do service in the Sanctuary, N.iv.47. We must
conclude, then, that the Levites were not involved in the general
doom; and, in fact, it is repeatedly said, N.ii.33, xxvi.62, that
they were not numbered among the 'children of Israel,' and the
doom in question is evidently confined to the 'children of
Israel,' except Joshua and Caleb. N.xiv.2,10, xxvi.62-65.

130. Now the population of England increases at the rate of
about 23 per cent. in ten years.*

Upon the same scale, then,—that is to say, at no *greater* rate
of increase than this,—the 22,000 Levites, (since these were
all the males of all ages, 'from a month old and upward,'
and therefore, may be reckoned as about half the whole mixed
population of Levites, male and female,) should have increased in ten years to 27,060, in the next ten years to 33,284,
in the next ten to 40,939, and in the last eight to 48,471,—
instead of which the number of this favoured tribe is given only
at 23,000. In other words, they *should* have increased by more
than 26,000; but they are represented as increased by only
1,000.

On the other hand, the tribe of Manasseh increased in the

* By the census of 1851, it was 17,892,149, and by that of 1861, 20,061,725,
besides 2,249,358 emigrants between March 31, 1851, and April 8, 1861. Some of
these emigrants would, of course, have died in the interval, if they had remained
in England. We may suppose that 2,000,000 would have survived, making
altogether the population in 1861, 22,061,725; so that the increase in 10 years
upon 17,892,149, was 4,169,676 or more than 23 per cent.

thirty-eight years from 32,200, N.i.35, to 52,700, N.xxvi.34, and all these were men in the prime of life, and not one of the 32,200 was numbered among the 52,700. Whereas the 22,000 Levites were males of all ages ' from a month old and upward,' and a large proportion of these, we may suppose, survived the thirty-eight years; and yet these, with their children and grand-children, were only increased by 1000 in the same interval.

131. It must now, surely, be sufficiently plain that the account of these numbers is of no statistical value whatever.

In fact, if we take the certain historical datum in (130, note), and assume that the Hebrew population increased, like that of England, at the rate of 23 per cent. in 10 years, then, reckoning the males as about half the entire population, we shall find that the 51 males in G.xlvi would have only increased in 215 years to 4,375* instead of 1,000,000. So, too, Dan's one son would have required 558 years to multiply to 104,500, the total number of Danite males existing at the time of the Exodus, according to N.ii.26, which we obtain by adding to the warriors there numbered the due proportion of old men and boys, as in (39).

132. But then what are we to say of the whole story of the Exodus, of the camping and marching of the Israelites, of their fighting with Amalek and Midian, of the 44 Levites (126) slay-ing 3,000 of the ' children of Israel,' E.xxxii.28, of their dying by pestilence, 14,700 at one time, N.xvi.49, 24,000 at another, N.xxv.9, as well as of the whole body of 600,000 fighting men being swept away during the forty years' sojourn in the wilder-ness? Several chapters of the book of Numbers are occupied in laying down the duties of the Levites, —not of the Levites, as they were to be in after years, when their numbers might

---

* The number in question will be represented mathematically by $61 (1 \cdot 23)^n$; and log. $51 + 21\frac{1}{2} \times$ log. $1 \cdot 23 = 1 \cdot 7075702 + 21\frac{1}{2} \times \cdot 0899051 = 3 \cdot 6405298 = $log.4,375.

be multiplied, but as they were to be then, in the wilderness, in attendance upon the Tabernacle. How were the 20 Kohathites, the 12 Gershonites, and the 12 Merarites, to discharge the offices assigned to them in N.iii,iv, in carrying the Tabernacle and its vessels,—to do, in short, the work of 8580 men, N.iv.48? What were these forty-four people, with the two Priests, and their families, to do with the forty-eight cities assigned to them, N.xxxv.7? How could the Tabernacle itself have been erected, when the silver spent upon it was contributed, as we are expressly told, by a poll-tax of half a shekel, E.xxxviii.26, levied upon the whole body of 603,550 warriors, who did not exist?

CHAPTER XIX.

133. In fact, the consequences of admitting the reality of the
above results are obviously so important, that, of course, the
most strenuous efforts have been made to ' reconcile' these dis-
crepancies, if possible, by those theologians, who support the
ordinary view, and who have studied the Pentateuch sufficiently
to be aware of the difficulties thus raised. The nature of the
attempt will be best seen, by simply stating the contrivances
resorted to for this purpose, to the sacrifice of all historical
truth and consistency.

Thus says Kurtz, ii.149, —

It is a gross mistake to suppose that the two millions were all the direct descendants of Jacob. When Jacob and his sons went down to Egypt, they must
certainly have taken with them all their menservants and maidservants, as well as
all their cattle. We know that Abraham had 318 servants, fit for war, and trained
to arms: his nomadic household must have contained, therefore, more than a thousand souls. Jacob, again, who inherited all these, brought with him from Syria so
many menservants and maidservants, and so much cattle, that, when he was afraid
of an attack from Esau, he divided them into two armies. With such data as
these, then, we are justified in assuming that the number of those, who went down
with Jacob into Egypt, was not limited to his sixty-six children and grand-children,
but consisted of several thousand menservants and maidservants. But, according
to G.xvii.12,13, these had all been circumcised; and in Egypt the descendants of
Jacob will, no doubt, have married the descendants of his servants. Hence we
regard the two million souls, who left Egypt at the Exodus, as the posterity of
the whole of the people, who went down into Egypt with Jacob.

It is very plain that Kurtz feels very much the necessity for

1

supposing the existence of these 'thousands' of ancestors, in order to produce the enormous population which he tries to account for.

134. We might answer in reply, as follows: —

(i) There is no word or indication of any such a cortège having accompanied Jacob into Egypt.

(ii) There is no sign even in G.xxxii,xxxiii, to which KURTZ refers, where Jacob meets with his brother Esau, of his having any such a body of servants.

(iii) If he had had so many at his command, it is hardly likely that he would have sent his darling Joseph, at seventeen years of age, to go, all alone and unattended, wandering about upon the veldt in search of his brethren.

(iv) These also are spoken of as 'feeding their flocks,' and seem to have had none of these 'thousands' with them, to witness their ill-treatment of their brother and report it to their father.

(v) Nothing is said about any of these servants coming down with the sons of Jacob to buy corn in Egypt, on either of their expeditions.

(vi) Rather, the whole story implies the contrary, — 'they speedily took down every man his sack to the ground, and opened every man his sack,' — 'then they rent their clothes, and laded every man his ass, and returned to the city,'—'we are brought in, that he may seek occasion against us, and take us for bondmen, and our asses,' not a word being said about servants.

(vii) In fact, their eleven sacks would have held but a very scanty supply of food for one year's consumption of so many starving 'thousands.'

(viii) The flocks and herds did not absolutely require any 'servants' to tend them, in the absence of Jacob's sons, since there remained at home, with the patriarch himself, his thirty-nine children and grand-children, as well as his sons' wives.

135. But, besides all this, it is evident that the whole stress of the story is laid upon this very point, that the multitude, — the *males*, at all events,—who went up out of Egypt at the Exodus, had come out of the loins of Jacob, and increased from the 'seventy souls,' who went down at first. If, then, we supposed that *all* the women were obtained from strangers, it is certain that the Pentateuch represents the 600,000 fighting men as Jacob's actual descendants, and 62,700 of these as the off-spring of Dan at the time of the Exodus. And we have the same difficulty as before, to explain how this could possibly have happened in 215 years and four generations.

136. But, says KURTZ, instead of 215 years, we must reckon 430 years, and the 'four generations' must mean '*four centuries.*' Even then, he admits the increase would be 'unparalleled in history.' Even then also there would remain other insuperable difficulties, as, for instance, that connected with the question of the firstborn (93), namely, that every Hebrew mother must have had, on the average, more than forty children.

But here the genealogies of Moses and Aaron, and the others quoted in (109), come in the way, and show distinctly what is meant by the 'fourth generation.' And the ages of Kohath and Amram are both given, so as to make it impossible, as we have seen (102), to extend the sojourn in Egypt to 430 years.

137. Then, KURTZ suggests, in the pedigree of Moses and Aaron there must be some names omitted.

The four members which commonly appear, Levi, Kohath, Amram, Moses, are intended merely to represent the four generations, who dwelt in Egypt. And this is the reason why the ages are given, and not to enable us to calculate how long the Israelites were in Egypt, which they would never enable us to do. II.141.

The meaning of the last clause in the above quotation is to me incomprehensible. But, as the pedigree of Moses and Aaron is repeated again and again, in a very precise and formal manner, without the least intimation being given that it is meant to be less historically true than any of the other genealogies, we must accept it as it stands. And, indeed, it would be strange, that we should have accurate genealogies given us for a number of persons of very second-rate importance in the story, and none at all for Moses and Aaron. And, even if we supposed that some names may have been omitted in this particular genealogy, how is it that so many other genealogies, as quoted in (109), contain only the same number of names? Besides, it is expressly stated, as a matter of *bonâ fide* domestic history, (as much so as that of Abraham marrying Sarah, or Isaac, Rebekah, or Jacob, Leah and Rachel,) that Amram married

I 2

'Jochebed his father's sister,' E.vi.20, 'the daughter of Levi, whom (his wife) bare to Levi in Egypt,' N.xxvi.59.

138. But then, says KURTZ, the word here rendered 'father's sister ' may only mean ' blood-relative on the father's side.' And there is *one* instance in the Scripture, (Jer.xxxii.12 compared with *v.*7,) where the Hebrew word seems to be used in this sense, though the other is the common and proper one.

Jochebed, then, may be called a ' daughter of Levi ' in the same sense in which Christ is called a 'son of David.' And this very phrase itself, ' whom (his wife) bare to Levi in Egypt,' has the appearance of a gloss appended to the preceding words 'daughter of Levi,' which the author of the gloss seems to have understood in their literal sense, as denoting an actual daughter of Levi, and then to have endeavoured to soften down the improbability of Moses' mother being a daughter of Levi, [as no daughter of Levi is mentioned in G.xlvi,] by appending a clause to the effect that the daughter in question was born in Egypt. This gloss, we admit, must have been introduced at a very early period, as it is found in every codex and version. ii.142.

But, even if these words are a gloss, and Jochebed was not an actual daughter of Levi, (which, however, is a mere conjecture of the above commentator,) the main fact would remain the same, viz. that the pedigree of Moses and Aaron is undoubtedly meant to be understood as a *bonâ fide* pedigree. And, as we have seen, it brings with it, as a necessary consequence, a number of absolute impossibilities,—among others, that six men must have had between them 2,748 sons (127).

139. Accordingly we find KURTZ himself almost driven to despair in his attempt to get over this difficulty:

Are we to believe, then, that Kohath's descendants through Amram consisted of no more than 6 males at the time of the census recorded in N.iii, (viz. Moses and his two sons, Aaron and his two sons,) whilst his descendants through the other three sons, Izhar, Hebron, and Uzziel, consisted at the very same period of 8,656 males [? 8,594, N.iii.28] at the very same time, that is, 2,885 for each ? This, certainly, is a *large* demand upon our faith. Still, as we cannot say that it is impossible, we submit and believe. But we are further required to believe, N.iii.27, that at this census the 6 Amramites — what am I saying ? there could really have been only *two* included in the census, namely, the two sons of Moses; for Aaron and his sons were Priests, to whom the Levites were to be assigned as a present ;

and, as it was for this very purpose that the census was taken, they would certainly not be included in it, any more than Moses himself; —hence, then, we are required to believe that the two remaining Amramites formed a distinct family, with precisely the same privileges and duties, as the 2,885 Izharites, the 2,885 Hebronites, and the 2,885 Uzzielites. We must candidly confess that our faith will not reach so far as this. ii.145.

140. KALISCH treats this matter as follows, *Exod.p.*160 : —

'It has often been considered questionable, if not impossible, that the seventy souls, who immigrated into Egypt in the time of Jacob, should, during their sojourn there, have increased to such a great nation. To explain this apparent difficulty, we remind the reader of the following facts and arguments.

(i) ' Among the Hebrews, like other nations, *polygamy was the rule.*'

Ans. Assumed without proof, and, if true, only aggravating enormously one of the main difficulties of the story (91.i.), in order to relieve which, KURTZ, as we have seen, assumes, with equal absence of proof, the *rarity* of polygamy among them.

(ii) 'They married early, as it is still customary in the East to enter the conjugal life in the thirteenth or fourteenth year.

(iii) ' They lived longer, and, no doubt, attained in the average to an age above ninety years.

(iv) ' By a singular Providence of God, they were not weakened by pestilence or famine.

(v) ' The prodigious fruitfulness of the Hebrews in Egypt is expressly mentioned in E.i.7.'

Ans. To the above we reply that, notwithstanding these early marriages, long lives, and great fruitfulness, the 12 sons of Jacob in G.xlvi had, on the average, only 4½ sons, and the Levites in E.vi only 3 sons; nor is there a single indication in the whole story that the Hebrew families were, generally larger than this. We have allowed fully for (iv) by supposing that all the sons in each family and generation lived on and multiplied.

(vi) 'The period, which elapsed, between the immigration of Jacob and the Exodus, amounts to 430 years. Now, if we take a generation to extend about 30 years, and suppose that, on the average, every man had no more than three sons, the 69 souls, excluding Jacob, trebled in 30 years; this number was again increased threefold in another 30 years; and, in 14 generations (420 years), they would, according to this calculation, amount to about 33 millions; and, therefore, no reasonable critic will find the number of 2½ millions impossible or exaggerated.'

Ans. We have shown that the number of years, according to the story, was 215, instead of 430, and the number of generations *four*, instead of *fourteen*. But,

Independently of these, there remains the difficulty of Levi's descendants, and of the number of the first-born.

141. RAWLINSON also, *Aids to Faith*, p.279-282, discusses this question of the 'sojourn in Egypt,' in relation to the numbers of the Israelites at the beginning and end of it. But, as usual, he only treats of the matter in its most general form, and does not touch upon the details,—such as the numbers of the tribe of Dan (125), or the descendants of Levi (127), or the number of first-borns (93),—which exhibit so distinctly the unhistorical character of the whole account. The only inference, that can be drawn from his silence on these points, is that he has not thoroughly, in his own person, considered this particular question, and has not really perceived these special difficulties at all, though they lie upon the very surface,— more especially as he writes,—

It is more easy to make a vague and general charge of absurdity against an adversary, than to point out in what the absurdity, with which he is taxed, consists.

142. With respect to the general question, however, RAWLINSON writes as follows : —

'No one asserts it to be naturally probable that such a company as went down with Jacob into Egypt would in 215, or even 430, years have become a nation possessing 600,000 fighting men. Orthodox commentators simply say that such an increase of numbers was *possible*, even in the shortest of these terms. They note that, if Jacob brought into Egypt 51 grandsons, and if, under the special blessing of God, so repeatedly promised to Abraham, his male descendants had continued to increase *at the same rate*, they would long within the specified periods, have reached the required number.'

Ans. We have shown in (118) that, *at the same rate of increase* as in Galvi, the number of warriors in the fourth generation, that of Joshua or Eleazar, would be only 4,923, instead of 600,000; while (124) *at the same rate of increase* as in Eri, it would only amount to 1377.

'In point of fact, they would in the *fifth* generation have exceeded 850,000, and in the *ninth* have amounted to 6,000,000.'

Ans. At the same rate of increase the number in the fifth generation would be 22,164 (or 4,131), and in the sixth, 99,693 (or 12,393). And, if the males of all the six generations were added together, their number would be only 126,156 (or 18,661), instead of exceeding 1,000,000.

143. The reader must be curious to know by what ingenious process RAWLINSON has contrived to produce such enormous numbers instead of the true ones. The solution of the mystery is given in the following extraordinary note.

'The average increase of the males in the generations had been *more than seven-fold* (!) each generation. A sevenfold increase would have given 857,157 males in the *fifth* generation, and 6,000,099 in the *sixth*.'

That is to say, because one man Jacob had 53, or more than seven-times seven, grandsons, therefore we are justified in assuming that his progeny was increased more than sevenfold in *each* generation! — it being left out of consideration altogether that —

(i) Though Jacob had twelve sons, yet these twelve had only fifty-three between them.

(ii) If Jacob's 12 sons be added to these 53, there will be only 65 sons and 13 parents, or an average of *five* sons for each.

(iii) The descendants of Levi are traced completely down to the fourth generation, and these on the average had only *three* sons each.

(iv) The Scripture states that there were 600,000 warriors in the *fourth* generation from Jacob's *sons*, whereas RAWLINSON's *fifth* and *sixth* generations are reckoned from Jacob's *grandsons*, and correspond, therefore, to the *sixth* and *seventh* of the Bible.

(v) Even at a seven-fold rate of increase, the males descended from Dan's one son would only have amounted to 313 warriors in the *fourth* generation, according to the Bible, 2,401 in the *fifth*, 16,807 in the *sixth*, — instead of being 62,700 in the *fourth*.

144. But the Essayist proceeds as follows : —

At the same time, as we are bound not to exaggerate the Divine interference with the ordinary course of nature, beyond what is actually stated or implied in Scripture, [hence we have no right to exceed the average of 4½ or, rather, 3 sons for each father], it ought to be borne in mind that we have no need to suppose the 600,000 fighting men, who quitted Egypt, though they are all called Israelites, to have been all descendants of Jacob. The members of the patriarch's family came down into Egypt *with their households*. What the size of patriarchal households was, we may gather from that of Abraham, whose 'trained servants born in his house' amounted to 318. Nor was this an exceptional case. Esau met Jacob, on his return from Padan-Aram, with 400 men, who were probably his servants; and Jacob, at the same meeting, had such a number, that he could divide them into two 'bands' or 'armies.' It is not unlikely that the whole company, which entered Egypt with Jacob, amounted to above a thousand souls. Kurtz thinks they must have consisted of 'several thousands.' As all were circumcised, all would, doubtless, be considered Israelites; and their descendants would be reckoned to the tribes of their masters.'

Ans. The reply to this argument is given in (131.135).

'Again, we must remember that polygamy prevailed among the Hebrews, and that, though polygamy, if a nation lives by itself, is *not* favourable to rapid increase, yet, if foreign wives can be obtained in any number, it is an institution, by means of which population may be greatly augmented.'

Ans. There is no indication that polygamy *did* 'prevail' among the Hebrews of those days. If it did, it aggravates the difficulty as to the first-borns (94.f). But, whether it did or not, the average number of sons for each father can only be reckoned, according to the Scripture data, as 4½ or, rather, 3.

'Egypt, moreover, was a country, where, both men and animals are said to have been remarkably prolific,—where, therefore, natural law would have tended in the same direction as the special action of Divine Providence at this time.'

Ans. But the fecundity of Egypt will not explain the difficulty as to Dan's descendants (125.143.v).

'These considerations do not, indeed, reduce the narrative within the category of ordinary occurrences; but they diminish considerably from its extraordinariness. They show that at any rate there is no need to extend the period of the sojourn beyond the 430 years of the Hebrew text, unless we seek to deprive the increase of that special and exceptional character, which is markedly assigned to it by the sacred historian.'

Ans. RAWLINSON, it seems, adopts, with KURTZ, the notion of the sojourn of the Israelites in Egypt lasting 430, instead of 215, years. We have shown that the *latter* is the Scripture statement, but that, on *either* supposition, the difficulties of the story are insuperable (136).

145. Lastly, this is HÄVERNICK'S account of the matter: *Pent.p.*240 : —

The number of the Israelites at the Exodus amounted to 600,000 men of war, which supposes the nation to have numbered *two millions and a half* of individuals. Now, while expressly regarding this extraordinary increase as a special divine blessing, and recognising in it also, in surveying the history from a higher point of view, the undeniable working of Providence, which in this manner would cause the liberation of Israel to appear the more splendidly as a divine act, yet natural causes also admit of being stated, as concurring to its production, and serving to explain the circumstance.

(i) The ample period of 430 years must certainly be regarded in the first place.

[To this remark, the translator, A. THOMSON, A.M. Prof. *Bibl. Lit. Glasgow Theol. Acad.*, appends very properly the note, 'This certainly appears to be an error.']

(il) We must next take into account the uncommon fruitfulness of Egypt, on which all the ancient authors are agreed, while they extol the peculiarly prosperous births of Egyptian women. This must especially be supposed to have been the case in the districts inhabited by the Hebrews, since there was the fruitfulness of the ground in addition. [See 140.v.*Ans.*]

(lii) There is no force at all in the objection that so many men could not have found room there. In the time of JOSEPHUS, *Jewish War*, ii.16, Egypt, exclusive of Alexandria, numbered seven millions of inhabitants; and yet, at that time, the population of the interior must have considerably diminished, if we compare the accounts of the ancients concerning Thebes in particular. [We have not advanced this want of room as an objection. It is plain, however, that HÄVERNICK has only regarded the question very superficially, and is not at all aware of the many difficulties by which it is surrounded.]

CHAPTER XX.

146. The book of Leviticus is chiefly occupied in giving directions to the Priests for the proper discharge of the different duties of their office, and further directions are given in the book of Numbers.

(i) In the case of 'every *burnt-offering*, which any man shall offer,' whether bullock, or sheep, or goat, or turtle-dove, 'the *Priests, Aaron's sons*, shall sprinkle the blood upon the altar, and put fire upon the altar, and lay the wood in order on the fire, and lay the parts, the head and the fat, in order upon the wood ;' and 'the *Priest* shall burn all on the altar, to be a burnt-sacrifice.' L.i.

(ii) So in the case of a *meat-offering*, L.ii, *peace-offering*, L.iii, *sin-offering*, L.iv, or *trespass-offering*, L.v,vi, the *Priest* has special duties assigned to him, as before.

(iii) Every woman after childbirth is to bring a lamb for a burnt-offering, and a pigeon or turtle-dove for a sin offering, or two young pigeons for the two offerings, and the *Priest* is to officiate, as before, L.xii.

(iv) Every case of leprosy is to be brought again and again to the *Priest*, and carefully inspected by him till it is cured, L.xiii.

(v) Any one, cured of leprosy, is to bring a burnt-offering and a sin-offering, and the *Priest* is to officiate, as before, L.xiv.

(vi) For certain ceremonial pollutions, which are specified, the *Priest* is to offer sacrifices, L.xv.15,30.

(vii) For a male or female Nazarite, when the days of separation are fulfilled, the *Priest* is to offer a burnt-offering, a sin-offering, and a peace-offering, N.vi.

(viii) Every day, morning and evening, the *Priest* is to offer a lamb for a continual burnt-offering, besides additional sacrifices on the Sabbath, the New Moon, at the Feast of Unleavened Bread, and at the Feast of the First-fruits, N.xxviii.

(k) In the seventh month, for several days together, besides the daily sacrifice, there were to be extraordinary additional sacrifices, so that on the fifteenth day of the month the Priest was to offer 13 bullocks, 2 rams, and 14 lambs, and in the seven days, from the fifteenth to the twenty-first, 70 bullocks, 14 rams, and 98 lambs. N.xxix.

(x) Lastly, if it should be thought that the above sacrificial system was not meant to be in full operation in the wilderness, we may call attention to the frequent references made, in the enunciation of these laws, to the Camp, Lev.12,21, vi.11,xiii.46,xiv.3,8, as well as to the words of the prophet Amos, v.25,—'Have ye offered unto Me sacrifices and offerings in the wilderness forty years, O House of Israel?'—which show that, in the prophet's view, at all events, such sacrifices were required and expected of them.

147. And now let us ask, for all these multifarious duties, during the forty years' sojourn in the wilderness, — for all the burnt-offerings, meat-offerings, peace-offerings, sin-offerings, trespass-offerings, thank-offerings, &c., of a population like that of the city of London, besides the daily and extraordinary sacrifices, — how many Priests were there?

The answer is very simple. There were only *three*, — Aaron, (till his death,) and his two sons, Eleazar and Ithamar.

And it is laid down very solemnly in N.iii.10, 'Thou shalt appoint Aaron and his sons, and they shall wait in the Priest's office; and *the stranger, that cometh nigh, shall be put to death.*' So again, v.38, 'Aaron and his sons, keeping the charge of the Sanctuary, for the charge of the children of Israel; and *the stranger, that cometh nigh, shall be put to death.*'

148. Yet how was it possible that these two or three men should have discharged all these duties for such a vast multitude? The single work, of offering the double sacrifice for women after child-birth, must have utterly overpowered three Priests, though engaged without cessation from morning to night. As we have seen (74) the births among two millions of people may be reckoned as, at least, 250 a day, for which, consequently, 500 sacrifices (250 burnt-offerings and 250 sin-offerings) would have had to be offered daily. Looking at the directions in Lev.i,iv, we can scarcely allow less than *five minutes* for each sacrifice; so that

these sacrifices alone, if offered separately, would have taken 2,500 minutes or nearly 42 hours, and could not have been offered in a single day of twelve hours, though each of the three Priests had been employed in the one sole incessant labour of offering them, without a moment's rest or intermission.

149. It may, perhaps, be said that *many* such sacrifices might have been offered at the same time. This is, surely, somewhat contrary to the notion of a sacrifice, as derived from the book of Leviticus; nor is there the slightest intimation, in the whole Pentateuch, of any such heaping together of sacrifices ; and it must be borne in mind that there was but *one* altar, five cubits (about 9 feet) square, E.xxvii.1, at which we have already supposed all the three Priests to be officiating at the same moment, actually offering, therefore, upon the altar *three* sacrifices *at once*, of which the *burnt*-offerings would, except in the case of poor women, L.xii.8, be *lambs*, and not pigeons.

150. But then we must ask further, where could they have obtained these 250 'turtle-doves or young pigeons' daily, that is, 90,000 annually, *in the wilderness?* There *might* be *two* offered for each birth ; there *must*, according to the Law, be *one*, L.xii.6,8. Did the people, then, carry with them *turtle-doves* and *young pigeons* out of Egypt, when they fled in such haste, and so heavily laden, and as yet knew nothing of any such law? Or how could they have had them at all under Sinai?

151. It cannot be said that the laws, which require the sacrifice of such birds, were intended only to suit the circumstances of a later time, when the people should be finally settled in the land of Canaan. As to this point HÄVERNICK writes, evidently not perceiving the difficulty before us, but stating the truth, as it would appear to any ordinary reader, *Pent.p.290* : —

Others also of these legal appointments bear the decided mark of being framed at (? for) a time, when all the individuals of the nation were so situated as to be at no great distance from the Tabernacle. Uncleanness by an issue of blood, &c., and that of *women in childbed*, require to be removed and atoned for by the *personal* presentation of offerings in the Sanctuary, &c.

In fact, we have one of these commands, manifestly referring to their life in the wilderness, L.xiv, where, after it has been ordered that the Priest shall go out of the Camp to look at the leper, *v.*3, and that the leper duly cleansed shall 'after that come into the *Camp*, and shall tarry abroad out of his *tent* seven days,' *v.*8, and on the eighth day shall offer 'two he-lambs and one ewe-lamb, &c.,' *v.*10, it is added, *v.*21, 'And, if he be poor, and cannot get so much, then he shall take one lamb, &c., and *two turtle-doves* or *two young pigeons*, such as he is able to get.' Here the 'turtle-doves or young pigeons' are prescribed as a lighter and easier offering for the poor to bring; they are spoken of, therefore, as being *in abundance*, as being within the reach of every one, in the wilderness, under Sinai! It would seem to follow that such laws as these could not have been written by Moses, but must have been composed at a later age, when the people were already settled in Canaan, and the poor, who could not afford a lamb, could easily provide themselves with pigeons. In the desert, it would have been equally impossible for rich or poor to procure them.

152. It may be said, indeed, that the יוֹנָה בְּנֵי, 'young pigeons,' were birds of the wilderness. Thus we read in Ps.lv.6,7, 'And I said, Oh that I had wings like a *dove* (יוֹנָה); for then would I fly away, and be at rest. Lo then would I wander far off, and remain in the *wilderness* (מִדְבָּר);' so Jer.xlviii.28, 'O ye, that dwell in Moab, leave the cities, and dwell in the rock, and be like the *dove*, that maketh her nest *in the sides of the hole's mouth*;' and Ezvii.16, 'They that escape of them shall escape, and shall be on the mountains like *doves* of the *valleys*, all of them mourning, every one for his iniquity.' Yet the Psalmist, in Ps.lv.6,7, was hardly thinking of the 'great and dreadful' · desert of Sinai. He had, probably, in view the wilderness of

Judah, or some other wide extent of 'uncultivated, and comparatively barren, country, into which cattle are driven to feed,' (Ges. *Lex.* סְרֶר,) far from the common haunts of men; and the יוֹנָה might be found dwelling in the rocks or valleys of such a solitude as this.

153. The desert of Sinai, indeed, is also called סְרֶר, as in N.xx.4, D.viii.15, D.xxxii.10, Jer.ii.6. But in each of the above passages some expression is added to show the terrific character of the Sinaitic waste; thus in N.xx.4, 'Why have ye brought up the Congregation of Jehovah into this wilderness, that we and our *cattle* should die there? . . . neither is there any water to drink;' in D.viii.15, 'that great and terrible wilderness, wherein were fiery serpents, and scorpions, and drought, where there was no water;' in D.xxxii.10, 'He found him in a desert land (בְּאֶרֶץ מִדְבָּר), in the waste howling wilderness (יְשִׁמֹן)'; in Jer.ii.6, 'Where is Jehovah, that led us through the wilderness, through a land of deserts and of pits, through a land of drought and of the shadow of death?' It can scarcely be believed that the בְּנֵי יוֹנָה, even if they could have been found here at all, would have been so numerous, that they could be spoken of as common birds, within the reach of the poorest of the Congregation, and be offered at the rate of 90,000 a year.

154. Again we have in N.xviii.9–11, the following commands addressed to Aaron by Jehovah Himself:—

'Every oblation of theirs, every meat-offering of theirs, and every sin-offering of theirs, and every trespass-offering of theirs, which they shall render unto me, shall be most holy for thee and for thy sons. *In the most holy place shalt thou eat it; every male shall eat it;* it shall be holy unto thee.

'This also is thine, the heave-offering of their gift, with all the wave-offerings of the children of Israel. I have given them unto thee, and to thy sons, and to thy daughters with thee, by a statute for ever; every one that is clean in thy house shall eat of it.'

Then follow other directions, by which it is provided that the Priest should have also 'the best of the oil, and all the best of the wine, and of the wheat, the first-fruits of them, which they shall offer unto Jehovah,' and ' whatsoever is first ripe in the land ;' which laws we may suppose were intended only to be applied, when the people had become settled on their farms in the land of Canaan, as also the law, *v.*25–29, for their receiving also a tenth of the tithes of corn and wine and oil, which were to be given for the support of the Levites.

But in *v.*14–18 we have again these provisions : —

'Every thing devoted in Israel shall be thine. Every thing that openeth the matrix in all flesh, which they bring unto Jehovah, whether it be of men or beasts, shall be thine: nevertheless, the first-born of man shalt thou surely redeem, and the firstling of unclean beasts shalt thou redeem.

' But the firstling of a cow, or the firstling of a sheep, or the firstling of a goat, thou shalt not redeem; they are holy: thou shalt sprinkle their blood upon the altar, and shalt burn their fat for an offering made by fire, for a sweet savour unto Jehovah.

' *And the flesh of them shall be thine, as the wave-breast and as the right shoulder are thine.*'

Similar directions are also laid down in L.vii : —

' As the sin-offering is, so is the trespass-offering; there is one law for them : the Priest, that maketh atonement therewith, shall have it. And the Priest, which offereth any man's burnt-offering, even the Priest shall have to himself the skin of the *burnt*-offering, which he hath offered. And all the meat-offering that is baked in the oven, and all that is dressed in the frying-pan and in the pan, shall be the Priest's that offereth it. And every meat-offering, mingled with oil, and dry, shall all the sons of Aaron have, one as much as another.' *v.*7–10.

' For the wave-breast and the heave-shoulder have I taken of the children of Israel from off the sacrifices of their peace-offerings, and have given them unto Aaron the Priest and unto his sons, by a statute for ever, from among the children of Israel.' *v.*34.

155. These last directions are given in the story before Aaron and his sons were consecrated. Hence they must be considered as intended to apply to them, while the Camp was in the wilderness, as well as to the ' sons of Aaron ' in future generations. But what an enormous provision was this for Aaron and his four, afterwards two, sons, and their families ! They were to have the skins of the *burnt*-offerings, and the

shoulder and breast (that is, double-breast) of the *peace-offerings*, of a congregation of two millions of people, for the general use of their three families! But, besides these, they were to have the whole of the *sin-offerings* and *trespass-offerings*, except the suet, which was to be burnt upon the Altar, L.iv.31,35,v.6, and the whole of the *meat-offerings*, except a handful, to be burnt as a memorial, L.ii.2; and all this was to be eaten *only by the three males, in the most holy place*, N.xviii.10!

156. And it would seem that they were not at liberty to *burn* the sin-offerings, or consume them in some other way than by eating: they must be 'eaten in the holy place.' At all events, we find it recorded that Moses, on one occasion, 'diligently sought the goat of the sin-offering, and, behold, it was burnt! and he was angry with Eleazar and Ithamar, the sons of Aaron, saying, Wherefore have ye not eaten the sin-offering in the holy place, seeing it is most holy, and God hath given it you to bear the iniquity of the Congregation, to make atonement for them before Jehovah? *Ye should indeed have eaten it in the holy place*, as I commanded.' L.x.16-20.

The very pigeons, to be brought as *sin-offerings* for the birth of children, would have averaged, according to the story, 264 a day; and each Priest would have had to eat daily 88 for his own portion, ' in the most holy place '!

157. HENGSTENBERG himself, *Pent.*ii.*p.*60, recognises, unawares, the force of the above argument, when he insists upon there having been a multitude of Priests in attendance on the Tabernacle in *Eli's* time, besides Eli himself and his two sons, Hophni and Phinehas.

Let it be considered that an extensive supply of Priests and sacrifices was required by the great reverence, in which, according to 1S.iv-vii, the Ark of the Covenant was held at this period. In the address of the man of God to Eli, 1S.ii.28, it is represented as the prerogative of the Priesthood to place the sacrifices on the Altar, to burn incense, and to receive all the offerings made by fire of the children of Israel. An order, possessed of such prerogatives, must have been held in high esteem, and must have contained a considerable number of members. *For what could one or two isolated Priests do with the sacrifices of all Israel?*

And again he writes, i.51 : —

Since *all* Israel at that time offered their sacrifices at the Sanctuary in Shiloh, *how was it possible for two or three Priests to perform the requisite service?*

HENGSTENBERG does not appear to see how strongly this argument bears against the historical veracity of the Pentateuch itself. For, if it was impossible for two or three Priests to suffice at Shiloh, for the Israelites who lived scattered about the land of Canaan, and who, therefore, could not possibly have *all* come continually to offer sacrifice, how was it possible for Aaron and his two sons to have 'performed the requisite service' for the whole assembled host in the wilderness?

158. Further, in Jo.xxi, we have an account of the forty-eight Levitical cities; and we read v.19, ' All the cities of the children of Aaron, the Priests, were thirteen cities, with their suburbs.'

At this time, according to the story, there was certainly one *son* of Aaron, Eleazar, and one grandson, Phinehas, and his family. Ithamar, Aaron's other son, *may* have been alive ; but no mention whatever is made of him. We may suppose, however, that he had sons and daughters. For this small number of persons, then, there are provided here *thirteen* cities and their suburbs, and all, let it be observed, *in the immediate neighbourhood of Jerusalem*, where the *Temple* was built, and where the presence of the Priests was especially required, but *in a later age*. SCOTT notes as follows : —

The family of Aaron could not at this time have been very numerous (!), though it had increased considerably (!) since his appointment to the Priesthood. Yet thirteen cities were allotted to it as a patrimony, in the divine knowledge of its future enlargement. For we have reason to think that no other family increased so much in proportion. after Israel's departure from Egypt, as that of Aaron.

The only conceivable reason for so thinking is the fact now

before us, viz. that thirteen cities were assigned to them. We do not find the sons of Aaron numerous in the time of the Judges, or in Eli's time, or Samuel's, or David's, or Solomon's, (except, indeed, in the record of the Chronicler). Aaron himself had at most only *two* sons living, and one of these had only *one* son.

CHAPTER XXI.

159. AGAIN, how did these three Priests manage at the celebration of the Passover?

We are told, 2Ch.xxx.16,xxxv.11, that the people killed the Passover, but '*the Priests sprinkled the blood from their hands and the Levites flayed them.*' Hence, when they kept the second passover under Sinai, N.ix.5, where we must suppose that 150,000 lambs (70) were killed at one time '*between the two evenings,*' E.xii.6, for the two millions of people, each Priest must have had to sprinkle the blood of 50,000 lambs in about two hours, that is, at the rate of about *four hundred lambs every minute for two hours together.*

Besides which, in the time of Hezekiah and Josiah, when it was desired to keep the Passover strictly, '*in such sort as it was written,*' 2 Ch.xxx.5, the lambs were manifestly killed *in the Court of the Temple.* We must suppose, then, that the Paschal lambs in the wilderness were killed *in the Court of the Tabernacle,* in accordance, in fact, with the strict injunctions of the Levitical Law, that all burnt-offerings, peace-offerings, sin-offerings, and trespass-offerings, should be killed '*before Jehovah,*' at the door of the Tabernacle of the Congregation.

160. Thus we read in the case of a burnt-offering, L.i.3,5,—

'He shall offer it of his own voluntary will at the door of the Tabernacle of the Congregation. And he shall kill the bullock *before Jehovah*; and the Priests,

R 2

Aaron's sons, shall bring the blood, and sprinkle the blood round about upon the Altar, that is by the *door of the Tabernacle of the Congregation.*'

So in the case of a peace-offering, L.iii.2,—

'He shall lay his hand upon the head of his offering, and kill it at the *door of the Tabernacle of the Congregation*; and Aaron's sons, the Priests, shall sprinkle the blood upon the Altar round about.' See L.i.3,5,11,15, iii.2,8,13,iv.4,6,&c.

Besides all which, we have this most solemn command, laid down in L.xvii.2-6, with the penalty of *death* attached for disobedience.

'This is the thing which Jehovah hath commanded, saying, What man soever there be of the House of Israel, that *killeth* an ox, or *lamb*, or goat, in the Camp, or that killeth it out of the Camp, and *bringeth it not unto the door of the Tabernacle of the Congregation,* to offer an offering unto Jehovah, blood shall be imputed unto that man, he hath shed blood, and *that man shall be cut off from among his people*; to the end that the children of Israel may bring their sacrifice, which they offer in the open field, even that they may bring them unto Jehovah, *unto the door of the Tabernacle of the Congregation, unto the Priest,* and offer them for peace-offerings unto Jehovah. And *the Priest shall sprinkle the blood upon the Altar of Jehovah, at the door of the Tabernacle of the Congregation,* and burn the fat (*suet*) for a sweet savour unto Jehovah.'

161. How, in fact, could the Priests have sprinkled the blood at all, if this were not the case, that the animals were killed in the Court of the Tabernacle?

But the area of that Court contained, as we have seen (38), only 1,692 square yards, and could only have held, when thronged, about 5,000 people. How then are we to conceive of 150,000 lambs being killed within it, by, at least, 150,000 people, in the space of two hours, — that is, *at the rate of 1,250 lambs a minute?*

162. I will here copy at full length, and consider carefully, the remarks of KURTZ upon these difficulties. iii.211-214 : —

'It is by no means an easy matter to picture to one's self the plan pursued in the celebration of this, the first, memorial-feast of the Passover, N.ix.5. The difficulty arises from the small number of Priests who could be employed. There were only three left after the death of Nadab and Abihu, viz. Aaron, Eleazar, and Ithamar.

Now, if we assume that all the lambs were slain at the Sanctuary, according to the injunction contained in D.xvi.2,5,6, and consider further that but a *very few* (two [*]) hours were set apart for the slaughter of the lambs, whilst, according to the laws of sacrifice, which were then in force, the sprinkling of the blood, at all events, was to be performed by the Priests, it might be thought that the number of Priests, whose services could be obtained, would hardly suffice for the work to be done.

'For, if we suppose the people to have numbered about two million souls, and reckon on an average one lamb to every fifteen or twenty persons, (*the proportion laid down in* E.xii.4,) there must have been from 100,000 to 140,000 lambs slain, and the blood sprinkled on the Altar,—a process for which neither the time allowed, nor the number of the Priests, can by any possibility have sufficed.'

Ans. There is no 'proportion' whatever laid down in Ex.xii.4. Josephus, as we have seen (70), reckons ten persons to each lamb. But Kurtz's own estimate will suffice for our present purpose. If there were only 120,000 lambs, it would follow that they would have had to be killed at the rate of 1,000 a minute, and each Priest, therefore, would have had to sprinkle the blood of 333 lambs a minute for two hours together.

'But are we justified in making such an assumption? It is nowhere stated that, on the occasion of this first festival in commemoration of the Exodus, the lambs were slaughtered at the Sanctuary, or that their blood either was, or was to be, sprinkled upon the Altar; nor is there any notice of the services of the Priests being required. But does this silence give us a right altogether to deny that the work in question was performed by the Priests? In E.xxiii.17, it is commanded that, at the annual Feast of the Passover, all the men in Israel should 'appear before the *face* of Jehovah.' In D.xvi.2,5,6, it is expressly forbidden to slay the Paschal lamb anywhere else than at 'the place, which Jehovah shall choose to place His Name there.' And, according to 2Ch.xxx.16, xxxv.11, though it is nowhere expressly commanded in the Pentateuch, the blood of all the Paschal lambs was sprinkled on the Altar by the Priests. At the same time there is certainly good ground for questioning whether the same course was adopted, in all respects, in connection with the Passover at Sinai.'

---

[*] Kurtz allows, II.301, that the Caraites and Samaritans are right in explaining the expression 'between the two evenings' to mean 'the period between the disappearance of the sun below the horizon and the time when it is quite dark, that is, from six o'clock till about half-past seven. Thus the first evening begins with the disappearance of the sun, the second with the cessation of daylight. Aben-Ezra gives the same explanation.'

Hence the time allowed for the killing of the Passover was, in fact, the time of *twilight*, and cannot, therefore, have been more than two hours, as we have reckoned it. And so writes Josephus (*De Bell. Jud.* vi.9,3), 'They slay their sacrifices at the Passover from the ninth hour to the eleventh.'

Ans. Would there, however, have been any questioning at all upon this subject, but for the very great difficulties here raised?

'E.xxiii.17 and D.xvi.2,5,6, relate particularly to the time, when the Israelites would be scattered in the various cities of the Promised Land, and far removed from the Sanctuary.'

Ans. But, if they were required to ' appear before Jehovah,' when the Holy Place was so far away from their homes, surely, à *fortiori*, they were required to do so in the wilderness, when the Tabernacle was close at hand.

And, besides the command in D.xvi.2,5,6, here referred to, we have that already quoted from L.xvii.2-6, which expressly refers to the ' Camp.'

' And the passages in Chronicles refer to the reigns of the later kings, just before the destruction of the kingdom of Judah.'

Ans. On the first of these occasions it is expressly said, they had not kept the Passover 'of a long time in such sort as it was written,' 2Ch.xxx.5. So that all, that was done at this Passover, was meant to be done in express agreement with what 'was written.' If, then, there is no specific direction that the blood of the Paschal lambs should be sprinkled by the Priests, yet it was clearly understood, according to the Chronicler, by the Priests and Prophets of Hezekiah's time, that such was the Divine command in respect of the Passover, as well as in respect of every other sacrifice.

'These facts might lead us to suppose that the slaughter of the lambs did not take place at the Sanctuary, till after the Israelites had taken possession of the Holy Land; and the sprinkling of the blood on the part of the Priests was probably introduced at a still later period.'

Ans. But the difficulty, attending the slaughtering of so many lambs, in so small a space, in so short a time, would have been just the same, whether it took place when the Tabernacle was set up at Shiloh in the land of Canaan, Jo.xviii.1, or while it was still erected in the wilderness. And the sprinkling of the blood is enjoined in the case of any sacrifice of any kind, L.xvii.6.

' To such a supposition, however, there are by no means unimportant objections. For, if the slaughter of the lambs was to take place at the Sanctuary in the time of Joshua, it is difficult to see why this should not also have been the case in the time of Moses, seeing that the Tabernacle was already erected, and the services in connection with it were regularly performed. And, if the slaughter of the lambs was necessarily associated with the Sanctuary, the sprinkling of the blood appears to have been associated with it as a matter of course; for this alone could give significance to all the rest, and, according to all analogy, it must be done by Priestly hands.'

163. The candour of Dr. KURTZ is thus far apparent, though he is evidently struggling with a great difficulty, and hardly

knows how to master it. We shall now see the extraordinary effort which he makes to do so, in direct violation of the plain meaning of the Scripture.

'Let us look again, however, and a little more closely, at D.xvi. We have been led away by recent custom, and, in what we have already written, have interpreted it as commanding the Paschal lamb to be slain in the fore-court of the Tabernacle. But there is not a word to that effect. The passage is worded thus : ' Thou mayest not sacrifice the Passover *in any one of thy cities*, which Jehovah will give thee; but *at the place*, which Jehovah shall choose to place His Name in, there thou shalt sacrifice the Passover at even.' This place is *not* the Tabernacle, nor the fore-court of the Tabernacle, but the City (or the Camp), in the midst of which the Tabernacle was erected. The pilgrimage to this place, which is here enjoined, was required by the distance of the cities of the land in which Israel dwelt. By means of this pilgrimage, on the part of all the Israelitish men, to the city of the Sanctuary, the same state of things, which existed when all Israel lived in the immediate neighbourhood of the Sanctuary, was to be reproduced at least three times a year. Hence it was no violation of the precept in D.xvi, if every family killed its own lamb in its own *house* or *tent*; for, even in this case, the lamb was slain *at the Sanctuary*, seeing that the Camp, which surrounded the Tabernacle on all sides in the same manner as the fore-court, (though with a much larger circumference,) or the City, in the midst of which the Tabernacle was erected, was, as it were, a second and larger fore-court, which was also holy, though not in the same degree. It was commanded, it must be remembered, that everything unclean should be removed from the Camp.'

Ans. This is all pure conjecture, without a shadow of ground for it,—rather, in direct opposition to all the practice in later days, as shown in 2Ch.xxx,xxxv, and to the letter and spirit of all the directions in the book of Leviticus, where, as we have seen, it is expressly commanded, that all burnt-offerings, peace-offerings, sin-offerings, trespass-offerings, shall be killed 'at the *door of the Tabernacle of the Congregation*,' and the blood 'sprinkled upon the altar round about,' as well as to the general very solemn command, for all kinds of sacrifices, in L.xvii.2-6.

'The large number of lambs to be slain *imperatively demanded* that this second and more extensive fore-court should be provided for the slaughter of the Paschal lambs. For how could more than 100,000 lambs by any possibility have been killed, in so short a space of time, within an area of about 4,600 square yards, (rather 1,692 square yards, see (38)], which was the utmost extent of the actual fore-court ?'

Ans. The question is pertinent enough. The 'imperative demand,' however, is made only by the necessity of the case, arising from the utter impossibility of the story as told in the Pentateuch.

'We are brought to the conclusion therefore, that the Mosaic Law permitted the lambs to be killed in private houses, provided the houses were within the Camp or City, in which the Tabernacle was erected. The circumstance, which first led to this, ceased after the erection of the Temple, as the fore-court was then of incomparably greater extent ; and the custom of slaying all the lambs at the Temple, which we meet with in 2Ch.xxx,xxxv, may have been introduced, as soon as the Temple was built.'

Ans. That is to say, in order to explain away an insuperable difficulty, Kurtz supposes, without a shadow of support from the Scripture for so doing, that almost the very first act of Moses, after the Tabernacle had been erected, and the laws of Divine Service distinctly laid down with regard to it, was to sanction a direct breach of them, —especially of the law just quoted from L.xvii.2–6.

164. Kurtz now proceeds to consider the other difficulty.

'A far greater difficulty presents itself in the supposed sprinkling of the blood by the Priests. But what were the actual facts of the case ? When the Tabernacle was first instituted, it was commanded that the blood of the lambs should be smeared on the door-posts of the respective houses, E.xii.7.

'This command is nowhere expressly revoked or changed. We are of opinion, nevertheless, that the altered circumstances led, as a matter of course, after the erection of the Sanctuary, to the sprinkling of the blood on the Altar, in the place of smearing on the door-posts ; and the book of Chronicles shows that this was actually the custom.'

Ans. Certainly this command could not have been carried out, either in the desert, where the people lived in *tents*, and there were no door-posts to be smeared, or in the land of Canaan, when the males 'went up,' it is supposed, from year to year, to keep the Passover at the central Sanctuary, whether the Tabernacle of Moses or that of David, or, in later days, the Temple. But surely it is strange that a command, supposed to be Divine, should have had to be set aside, as impossible to be obeyed, on the very first occasion of the memorial Feast being celebrated, at the second Passover, under Sinai, and ever after, during the lifetime of that whole generation,—more especially as the Injunction in E.xii.24, 'And ye shall observe this thing for an ordinance to thee and to thy sons for ever,' seems to have express reference to this very ceremony, which had just been described in v.22,23. And so writes Kalisch, *Exod.*p.136,—

'According to tradition, this act of marking the door-posts was limited to the Passover in Egypt, and not repeated at its later celebrations, although *this appears to be against the clear instructions of Moses, v.7,22,24.*'

And again he observes, *Exod.*p.135,—

'It would appear from the context, v.23–27, that the eternal observance here enjoined refers to the marking of the door-posts with the blood of the Paschal lambs. However, the *traditional Jewish interpretation* (!) has applied it to the *general* precepts concerning the Passover, and limited that ceremony only to that one Passover in Egypt.'

At all events, we should have expected that some provision for this state of things would have been made, by Divine authority, at the first institution of the Passover, or, at least, that some intimation of so remarkable a modification of the original law would have been made at the second celebration.

'But the exceptional character of the Passover warrants the assumption, that, on every occasion, just as on the first celebration, the sprinkling of the blood might be performed by the head of the household himself. If this had not been the case, we should most likely have found some intimation in the account of the second Passover, N.ix., of the cooperation of the Priests. We are warranted, therefore, in adopting the conclusion, to which many other circumstances point (?), that, on the celebration of the Passover, the Priestly vocation, which, according to Exix.6, 'And ye shall be unto me a kingdom of Priests, and a holy nation,' originally belonged to all the Israelites, retained its validity as an exceptional case, *for the purpose of keeping in mind the calling,* which they had voluntarily declined from a consciousness of their weakness, 'Speak thou with us and we will hear; but let not God speak with us, lest we die,' Ex.xx.19,—the realisation of which was merely postponed, and not suspended altogether, and to the full possession of which they would certainly eventually attain. The outward warrant for the discharge of this exceptional Priestly function, on the occasion of the Passover, might possibly be found in the fact, that the words of Ex.xx.19 had not yet been spoken, that is to say, the suspension of the Priestly calling had not been solicited or granted, at the time when the Passover was first instituted.'

Ans. Can anyone suppose that, if these words had not been spoken, there would have been no 'suspension of the Priestly calling' of the Israelites, no Priests specially set apart for the service of the Tabernacle, no peculiar Priestly duties assigned to them, which others might not perform on pain of death, as laid down in the books of Leviticus and Numbers? Nay, before the above words were spoken, we actually read of 'the Priests, that come near to Jehovah,' Ex.ix.22: so that, whatever this last expression may mean, whoever these Priests may have been, (as the Aaronical Priesthood was not yet in existence), we must suppose that the idea of a Priesthood of some kind was already existing among them. It is certainly true that the references to the Priests in the books of Exodus and Numbers, do not appear to imply in any way that the Priests were called into action in the celebration of this Feast. But *that* very circumstance occasions one of the greatest of the difficulties, which are here presented. For how is this fact to be explained, in the face of the very solemn injunction quoted above (160) from Lxvil? What, therefore, Kurtz gains in one direction for the relief of his perplexity, by supposing the inaction of the Priests at the second and subsequent celebrations of the Passover, he loses in the other.

'It is true that the passages already quoted from the Chronicles prove that, at a later period, it was the custom for the blood to be sprinkled by the Priests, even on the occasion of the Passover. But this may have been one of the very numerous modifications, which were introduced into the worship, in consequence of the erection of the Temple.'

Ans. But Hezekiah desired to have the Passover kept strictly 'in such sort as it was written.' And, surely, it is preposterous to assume, on the one hand, as KURTZ does, that, after the first Passover, the blood was sprinkled on the *Altar* in the Court of the Tabernacle, at all events while the people lived in the wilderness, and then, on the other hand, to assume also that it was *not* sprinkled by the *Priests.* Can anything, in fact, be more plain than the language in 2Ch.xxx.16, 'And they stood in their place, after their manner, *according to the Law of Moses,* the man of God: the Priests sprinkled the blood, from the hand of the Levites?'

The truth is, that the difficulty, which exists in this part of the story of the Pentateuch, is as evident to KURTZ's eyes as it is to our own, though he cannot as yet bring himself to acknowledge it, as involving an impossibility.

CHAPTER XXII.

165. We have now concluded our preliminary work of pointing out some of the most prominent inconsistencies and impossibilities, which exist in the story of the Exodus as it lies before us in the Pentateuch; and we have surely exhibited enough, to relieve the mind from any superstitious dread, in pursuing further the consideration of this question. I believe that to the great majority of my readers many of the above facts will be new, as, I freely admit, they were to myself till within a comparatively recent period. It seems strange that this should be so; but the power of habit is great, or, as an able writer has otherwise expressed it from his own point of view, the Rev. A. W. HADDAN, *Replies to Essays and Reviews*, p.348,—

One has great faith in the mere *inertia* of religious belief.

166. But that the case is really as I have stated it, viz. that the Clergy and Laity of England generally have not had these facts before their eyes at all, is proved to my own mind most forcibly by the simple circumstance, that in neither of the two volumes, 'Aids to Faith' and 'Replies to Essays and Reviews,' both brought out under especial episcopal sanction, for the very purpose of settling the doubts, which might be raised in the minds of many by the suggestions of the Essayists, scarcely any reference whatever is made to any one of the above primary

difficulties, which beset the question of the historical accuracy of
the Mosaic story. In the latter volume, to which we were to look
for 'a calm, comprehensive, scholarlike declaration of positive
truth upon all the matters in dispute,' I find not the slightest
notice taken of any one of them; and a very large portion of
more than one of the 'Replies' is, as it appears to me, unpro-
fitably occupied in mere censure — not to say, abuse — of the
adversary. I opened this book with great interest, from the
names of the authors, and the high sanction under which it
had been issued, and eagerly sought in it for something of importance, bearing upon the question now before us. I must
confess to have put it down with a painful sense of disappoint-
ment.

167. On turning, however, to the other volume, 'Aids to
Faith,' I find Prof. RAWLINSON writing as follows, p. 252 : —

The authenticity of the Pentateuch has been recently called in question, principally on the following points : —

(i) The chronology, which is regarded as very greatly in deficiency;

(ii) The account given of the Flood, which is supposed to magnify a great
calamity in Upper Asia into a general destruction of the human race;

(iii) The ethnological views, which are said to be sometimes mistaken;

(iv) The patriarchal genealogies, which are charged with being purely my-
thical;

(v) The length of the lives of the patriarchs, which is thought to be simply
impossible;

(vi) *The duration of the sojourn in Egypt, which is considered incompatible with
the number of the Israelites on entering and quitting the country.*

Each of the above points will be found noticed in its proper
place in the course of this work. It will be observed, however,
that the above writer has in (vi) touched upon one, and only
one, of the serious questions, which have been discussed at
length in the foregoing pages, and even that, as we have seen
(141), he has treated only generally and superficially. The other
'principal points of objection,' which he considers, though not
without weight in themselves, are of no importance whatever in
reference to the present argument, which is already completed,

without our having had as yet occasion to enter upon any examination of them.

168. From the above considerations it surely follows, that the account of the Exodus of the Israelites, as given in the Pentateuch, whatever real foundation it may have had in the ancient history of the people, is mixed up, at all events, with so great an amount of contradictory matter, that it cannot be regarded as historically true, so as to be appealed to, as absolute, incontestable matter of fact, in Church formularies.

For, let it be observed, the objections, which have been produced, are not such as touch only one or two points of the story. They affect the entire substance of it, and, until they are removed, they make it impossible for a thoughtful person to receive, without further enquiry, any considerable portion of it, *as certainly true* in an historical point of view. It is plain that, in its own essential statements of matters of fact, the narrative of the Exodus is full of contradictions.

169. We cannot here have recourse to the ordinary supposition, that there may be something wrong in the *Hebrew numerals.* This suggestion will not avail here, however it might be applied in other cases to reduce within the bounds of probability the extravagant statements of Hebrew writers,—such as that in Ju.xii.(!, where we are told that the Gileadites under Jephthah slew of their brethren, the Ephraimites, 42,000 men,—or that in Ju.xx, where, first, the Benjamites slay of the Israelites, 40,000 men, v.21,25, and then the Israelites kill of the Benjamites 43,100, v.35,44, all these being 'men of valour,' that 'drew the sword,'—or that in 1S.iv.10, where the Philistines slew of Israel 30,000 footmen, or in 1S.xiii.5, where the Philistines had 30,000 war-chariots, or in 2S.x.18, where David slew of the Syrians 40,000 horsemen, or in 2Ch.xxviii.6,8, where Pekah, king of *Israel,* slew of *Judah* in one day 120,000 'sons of valour,' and carried away captive

200,000 'women, sons, and daughters,' or in 2Ch.xiii.3, where
Abijah's force consisted of 400,000, and Jeroboam's of 800,000,
and Judah slew Israel, v.17, ' with a great slaughter; so there
fell down slain of Israel 500,000 chosen men!!!'—it being
remembered that, at the battle of Waterloo, there were killed
of the allies, 'British, Germans, Hanoverians, Brunswickers,
men of Nassau, Belgians, and Prussians,' altogether only 4,172
men. (ALISON's *Hist. of Europe*, xlx.p.372.)*

170. But as regards the Pentateuch, not only is the number
'600,000 on foot, besides women and children,' given distinctly
in E.xii.37, at the time of their leaving Egypt; but we have it
recorded again, thrice over, in *different forms*, in E.xxviii.25-28,
at the beginning of the forty years' wanderings, when the
number of all that ' went to be numbered, from twenty years old

* So JOSEPHUS in his Autobiography, ch.6, states that the people of Scythopolis
fell upon the Jews, 'their fellow-citizens and confederates, and slew them all, being
in number many *ten thousands*. But,' he adds, 'we have given a more accurate
account of these things in the books of the Jewish War.' On turning to the Jewish
War, ii.18.3, we find the number stated as 'above 13,000.' Most probably, neither
statement is correct; and, in fact, JOSEPHUS's numbers are very frequently as extravagant and unreal as those of the Scripture writers. It is an idle, or, rather, it
is a sinful, paltering with the truth, to attempt to explain away so many cases of
this kind by supposing on every such occasion an error of a scribe. This might
avail to account for two or three such instances. But it is impossible for us not to
perceive that a systematic *habit* of exaggeration in respect of numbers prevails
among Hebrew writers of history, probably from not realising to their own minds
the actual meaning and magnitude of the numbers employed. And this is more
especially true of the Chronicler, witness the following statements which he makes
in the course of his narrative, besides those above quoted. Thus Asa's force consisted of 580,000, Zerah's of 1,000,000, 2Ch.xiv.8,9, Jehoshaphat's of 1,160,000,
'besides those whom the king put in all the fenced cities throughout all Judah,'
xvii.14-19; Amaziah marches against the Edomites, with 300,000, and hires
100,000 more out of Israel, xxv.5,6; Uzziah's force consisted of 307,500, xxvi.13.
The kingdom of Judah contained about 2,500 square miles, that is, in extent it was about half as large as the counties of Norfolk, Suffolk, and Essex
together; but in Jehoshaphat's time it contained, according to 2Ch. xvii.14-19,
1,160,000 warriors, that is, about 4,000,000 of inhabitants; in other words, it was
eight times as thickly peopled as the three Eastern Counties in the present day;
and yet a great part of Judah was very unfruitful.

and upward,' is reckoned at 603,550 ; and this is repeated again in N.i.46 ; and it is modified once more, at the end of the wanderings, to 601,730, N.xxvi.51. Besides which, on each occasion of numbering, each separate tribe is numbered, and the sum of the separate results makes up the whole.

Thus this number is woven, as a kind of thread, into the whole story of the Exodus, and cannot be taken out, without tearing the whole fabric to pieces. It affects, directly, the account of the construction of the Tabernacle, E.xxxviii.25-28, and, therefore, also the reality of the institutions, whether of the Priesthood or of Sacrifice, connected with it. And the multiplied impossibilities introduced by this number alone, independent of all other considerations, are enough to throw discredit upon the historical character of the whole narrative.

171. These things we have all along been looking at, as it were, from a distant point of view, through a misty atmosphere, dreading, it may be, some of us, to approach and gaze more closely upon the truth itself, which, once clearly seen, must dissipate many of our most cherished convictions, and hardly daring, indeed, to engage in (what so many would deem) an irreverent and impious undertaking. To those of my readers, however, who have followed me thus far, I hope it will now be apparent, that there is no longer any cause for superstitious terror, in respect of the enquiries which we are making,—rather that it is our bounden duty, as servants of God, the very God of Truth, and in dependence on His help and blessing, to pursue them yet farther, whatever the result may be, fearing no evil, for what shall harm us, if we are followers of that which is right, and good, and true ?

172. But how thankful we must be, that we are no longer obliged to believe, as a matter of fact, of vital consequence to our eternal hope, the story related in N.xxxi, where we are told that a force of 12,000 Israelites slew *all* the males of

144 THE WAR ON MIDIAN.

the Midianites, took captive *all* the females and children, seized
all their cattle and flocks, (72,000 oxen, 61,000 asses, 675,000
sheep,) and *all* their goods, and burnt *all* their cities, and *all*
their goodly castles,' without the loss of a single man,— and
then, by command of Moses, butchered in cold blood all the
women and children, ' except all the women-children, who have
not known a man by lying with him.' These last the Israelites
were to ' keep for themselves.' They amounted, we are told,
to 32,000, *v.*35, mostly, we must suppose, under the age of sixteen or eighteen. We may fairly reckon that there were as
many more under the age of forty, and half as many more
above forty, making altogether 80,000 females, of whom, according to the story, Moses ordered 48,000 to be killed, besides
(say) 20,000 young boys. The tragedy of Cawnpore, where
300 were butchered, would sink into nothing, compared with
such a massacre, if, indeed, we were required to believe it.
And these 48,000 females must have represented 48,000 men,
all of whom, in that case, we must also believe to have been
killed, their property pillaged, their castles demolished, and
towns destroyed, by 12,000 Israelites, who, in addition, must
have carried off 100,000 captives, (more than eight persons to
each man,) and driven before them 808,000 head of cattle,
(more than sixty-seven for each man,) and all without the loss
of a single man! How is it possible to quote the Bible as in any
way condemning slavery, when we read here, *v.*40, of ' Jehovah's
tribute ' of slaves, thirty-two persons?

173. But it may be well at once to show that, besides involving the above incredible statements, the narrative itself, as
it now stands, is unhistorical here as elsewhere.

(i) We are told that Aaron died on 'the *first* day of the *fifth* month' of the
fortieth year of the wanderings, N.xxxiii.38, and they mourned for him a month,
N.xx.29.
(ii) After this, ' king Arad the Canaanite fought against Israel, and took some
of them prisoners ; ' whereupon the Israelites attacked these Canaanites, and

utterly destroyed them and their cities,' N.xxi.1-3, — for which two transactions
we may allow another month.

(iii) Then they 'journeyed from Mount Hor, by the way of the Red Sea, to
compass the land of Edom,' N.xxi.4, and the people murmured, and were plagued
with fiery serpents, and Moses set up the serpent of brass, N.xxi.5-9, — for all
which we must allow, at least, a fortnight.

(iv) They now marched, and made nine encampments, N.xxi.10-20, for which
we cannot well allow less than a month.

'We believe that, at every station, at least three days' rest must have been
required.' Kcara.iii.p.231.

(v) Then they sent messengers to Sihon, who 'gathered all his people together,
and fought against Israel,' and ' Israel smote him with the edge of the sword,' and
'possessed his land from Arnon unto Jabbok,' and 'took all these cities, and dwelt
in all the cities of the Amorites, in Heshbon and in all the daughters thereof,'
N.xxi.21-26, — for which we may allow another month.

(vi) After that 'Moses sent to spy out Jaazer, and they took the villages thereof,
and drove out the Amorites that were there,' N.xxi.32,— say, in another fortnight.

(vii) Then they 'turned up by the way of Bashan, and Og, the king of Bashan,
went out against them, and they smote him, and his sons, and all his people, until
there was none left him alive, and they possessed his land.' N.xxi.33-35. For all
this work of capturing 'three-score cities, fenced with high walls, gates, and bars,
besides unwalled towns, a great many,' D.iii.4,5, we must allow, at the very least, a
month.

174. Thus, then, from the *first day of the fifth month,*' on
which Aaron died, to the completion of the conquest of Og, king
of Bashan, we cannot reckon less altogether than *six months,*
(and, indeed, even then the events will have been crowded one
upon another in a most astonishing, and really impossible,
manner,) and are thus brought down to the *first day of the
eleventh month,* the very day on which Moses is stated to have
addressed the people in the plains of Moab.   D.i.3.

And now what room is there for the other events, which are
recorded in the book of Numbers, as having occurred between
the conquest of Bashan and the address of Moses?   The chief
of these were —

(1) The march forward to the plains of Moab, N.xxii.1 ;

(2) Balak's sending twice to Balaam, his journey, and pro-
phesyings, xxii.2-xxiv ;

(3) Israel's 'abiding' in Shittim, and committing whoredom with the daughters of Moab, xxv.1-3;

(4) The death of 24,000 by the plague, xxv.9;

(5) The second numbering of the people, xxvi;

(6) The war upon Midian, above considered, during which they 'burnt all their cities, and all their goodly castles,' &c., and surely must have required a month or six weeks for such a transaction.

175. Another obvious inference from the above facts is that such a narrative as that of the Exodus could never, — in its present form, and as a whole, at all events, — have been written by Moses, or by any one who had actually taken part in the scenes which it professes to describe. As PLÄTZNICK observes, *Pent.* p.90 : —

If the Pentateuch would fully maintain its right to the position which it claims, as the work of Moses and the commencement of the sacred records of the covenant-people, it must fulfil the requisition of showing itself to be a work *historically true*, — containing a history which shall vindicate itself by critical examination, as maintaining invariably the character of perfect truth, in reference to the assumed period of its composition.

And so says HENGSTENBERG, *Pent.* ii.283 : —

It is the unavoidable fate of a spurious historical work of any length, to be involved in contradictions. This must be the case to a very great extent with the Pentateuch, if it be not genuine. . . . . If the Pentateuch is spurious, its histories and laws have been fabricated in successive portions, and were committed to writing in the course of centuries by different individuals. From such a mode of origination a mass of contradictions is inseparable, and the improving hand of a later editor would never be capable of entirely obliterating them. From these remarks it appears that freedom from contradictions is much more than the *conditio sine qua non* of the genuineness of the Pentateuch. . . . . It may be thought that Moses, in the history of *ancient* times, found contradictions, and repeated the tradition without removing them. Where, however, Moses narrates what he himself spoke, did, or saw, there every real contradiction becomes a witness against the genuineness.

CHAPTER XXIII.

176. WE shall next proceed, in the Second Part of this work, to consider the signs, which these books of the Pentateuch give, upon close inspection, of the *manner*, and of the *age* or *ages*, in which they have been composed.

But, meanwhile, I cannot but feel that, having thus been impelled to take an active part in showing the groundlessness of the popular notion of Scripture Inspiration, which so many have long regarded as the very foundation of their faith and hope, a demand may be made upon me for something to supply the loss, for something to fill up the aching void, which will undoubtedly be felt at first, where *that* faith, which has been built only or mainly upon the basis of the historical truth of the Pentateuch, must be in danger of collapsing, together with its support. In the present stage of the discussion, it is impossible for me to answer fully, as I would, to such a demand, though I trust to be enabled to do so before my work is brought to its close.

177. I would, however, venture to refer the reader, for some words, which, I would humbly hope, by GOD's Mercy, may minister in some measure to the comfort and support of troubled minds, under present circumstances, to my lately-published *Commentary on the Epistle to the Romans.* That Commentary, it is true, though *published* after I had formed my opinion

L 2

of the real nature of the Mosaic story, was written long
before, and the greatest part of it printed, at a time when I
had no idea of ever holding my present views. I believe that
I have rightly explained in it the Apostle's own meaning,
and have expressed truly, as it seems to me, the manner in
which he himself would have adapted his teaching to the
circumstances, social and intellectual, of the present day. The
main essence of that teaching is that our righteousness is
wholly of 'faith,' a living trust in God's Love, — that we
must all, and we may all, depend entirely on our Father's
Mercy, and come as children to His Footstool, continually, for
light and life, for help and blessing, for counsel and guidance,
and, if need be, for that 'loving correction,' which 'shall
make us great.' That essential principle of St. Paul's teaching
remains still an eternal Truth for our strength and consolation, whatever may be the effect of the view, taken of the
Mosaic history, upon other parts of the current belief of Christendom. Under any circumstances, should I have occasion to
reprint that book, I should only have to modify in some
places the form of the expression. The main substance of
the book,—those parts, which explain the Apostle's teaching,
and set forth the great principles, which that teaching involves, of a calm confiding trust in God's Fatherly Love, an
abiding sense of His Presence, a childlike desire and endeavour, by His own Good Spirit's help, to do His Will and
grow in His Likeness,—would need no change. And I enter-
tain the hope that views, such as those stated in that book,—
which during the last twenty years have been freely and fully
taught by master-minds,* within the pale of the Church of
England, and have taken strong hold upon the hearts of many,
—as they have enabled my own spirit to bear with more calm-

* I think it right to say that, in making and publishing such investigations,
as those which are contained in this book, I am neither guided by the example of
my friend, the Rev. F. D. Maurice, nor acting with his advice or approval.

ness, and stedfastness of faith in the Living God, the shock
which I experienced at first, on perceiving the unhistorical
character of the Mosaic narrative,—may be of like use to others,
and prepare their minds for yet wider and grander views of
God's dealings with Man, and with the Universe, than we have
yet attained to.

178. And it may be that the time is near at hand, in the
ordering of God's Providence, when the way shall be opened for
a wide extension of Missionary work among the heathen,—when
that work, which now languishes, which cannot make progress
among them, either among the ignorant Zulu or the learned
Hindoo, shall no longer be impeded by the necessity of our
laying down, at the very outset, stories like these for their reception, which they can often match out of their own traditions,
and requiring them, upon pain of eternal misery, to 'believe' in
them all 'unfeignedly,'—and when a Missionary Bishop of the
Church of England shall not be prevented, as I myself have been,
from admitting to the Diaconate a thoroughly competent, well-
trained, able and pious, native, who had himself helped to translate
the whole of the New Testament and several books of the Old,
because he *must* be ordained by the formularies of the Church of
England, and those require that he should not only subscribe to
the Thirty-nine Articles, and acknowledge the book of Common
Prayer,—parts of which, the nice distinctions of the Athanasian
Creed for instance, cannot possibly be translated into his
language,—but solemnly declare, in the presence of God and the
Congregation, that he 'unfeignedly believes *all* the Canonical
Scriptures,' some parts of which, as the genealogies in Chro-
nicles, and the books of Esther and Daniel, as well as large
portions of the prophecies, he had never read.

179. I cannot say that I felt a religious scruple myself about
ordaining a native candidate under such circumstances, without
requiring him to enter on his ministerial course by uttering a
falsehood, though aware that, by the thirty-sixth Canon, I

should, for ordaining him without such a precaution, have rendered myself liable to suspension. But others about me had scruples of this kind, and I deemed it best, under the circumstances, to defer to their judgment, until I could lay the matter before the Church at home. I do now lay it before the Church, though in a much wider form than I at first contemplated. And I trust that, as Ministers of God's Truth and God's Message of Love to mankind, we shall be able before long to meet the Mahomedan and Brahmin and Buddhist, as well as the untutored savage of South Africa and the South Pacific, on other and better terms than we now do, and no longer feel ourselves obliged to maintain every part of the Bible as an infallible record of past history, and every word as the sacred utterance of the Spirit of God.

180. This, however, it must be confessed, is the practice, in the present day, of most Protestant Missionaries, whether within or without the Church of England; while, on the other hand, I have been told distinctly, by one of themselves, that some foreign Missionaries do not think it expedient to put the Old Testament into the hands of natives at all. There are others, doubtless, in the Christian Ministry, who have attained to wider views of Scripture Inspiration, and who do not suppose that those narratives are historically true, and yet 'believe unfeignedly' in the Divine Authority of the Scriptures, relying on the records as an efficient instrument of communication from God to Man, in all that is 'necessary to salvation.' And the number of such believers, both among the Clergy and Laity, is probably increasing daily.

181. Meanwhile, in order that we may give due honour to the Bible, as containing a message from God to our souls, it is surely necessary that we take ourselves, in the first place, and teach others to take, a right and true view, both of the contents of the Book, and of the nature of its Inspiration. Then, instead of looking to it for revelations of scientific or historical facts,

which God has never promised to disclose in this way, by sudden
supernatural communications, without the use of human powers
of intellect, and without due labour spent in the search after
truth, we shall have recourse to it for that which God has there
in His Providence laid up in store for our use,—food for the
inner man, supplies of spiritual strength and consolation, living
words of power to speak to our hearts and consciences, and wake
us up to daily earnestness of faith and duty. That very Book
of Truth will then cheer us with the assurance of Divine help
and blessing, while we engage ourselves devoutly and faithfully in such a work as that which now lies before us, and
diligently exercise the best faculties of mind, which God
has given us, in searching into the true origin and meaning of the Bible narrative, and its relation to other facts of
science or history.

182. And this may be the step, which God in His Providence
calls us to take in the present age, in advance of the past generation, with reference to the subject now before us. In the time
of Galileo, it was heresy to say that the sun stood still, and the
earth went round it. In far later times, the days of the child-
hood of many now living, it was thought by many heresy to say
that the fossil bones, dug up within the earth, were not the
signs of Noah's Flood, or to maintain that death was in the
world, and pain, and multiplied destruction of living creatures
by fire and flood, millions of years before the first man had
sinned. Yet all these are now recognised as *facts*, which
cannot be disputed, which our very children should be taught to
know. And good men will even set themselves down to wrest
the plain meaning of the Scriptures themselves into a forced
conformity with these admitted results of modern science.

183. But, in this our day, by the Gracious Favour of the
'Father of Lights, the Giver of every good and perfect gift,'
other sciences, besides geology, have sprung into sudden growth,
and have attained already a wonderful developement. The

results of scientific criticism, applied to the examination of the
letter of the Scriptures, will also soon be acknowledged as *facts*,
which must be laid as the basis of all sound religious teaching.
In view of this change, which, I believe, is near at hand, and in
order to avert the shock, which our children's faith must otherwise experience, when they find, as they certainly will before
long, that the Bible can no longer be regarded as infallibly
true in matters of common history,—as we value their reverence
and love for the Sacred Book,—let us teach them at once to
know that they are not to look for the inspiration of the Holy
One, which breathes through its pages, in respect of any such
matters as these, which the writers wrote as men, with the same
liability to error from any cause as other men, and where they
must be judged as men, as all other writers would be, by the
just laws of criticism.

184. Let us rather teach them to look for the sign of God's
Spirit, speaking to them in the Bible, in that of which their own
hearts alone can be the judges, of which the heart of the simple
child can judge as well as—often, alas ! better than—that of the
self-willed philosopher, critic, or sage,— in that which speaks
to the witness for God within them, to which alone, under God
Himself, whose voice it utters in the secrets of his inner being,
each man is ultimately responsible,— to the Reason and Conscience. Let us bid them look for it in that within the Bible,
which tells them of what is pure and good, holy and loving, faithful and true, which speaks from God's Spirit directly to their
spirits, though clothed with the outward form of a law, or
parable, or proverb, or narrative,—in that which they will feel
and know in themselves to be righteous and excellent, however
they may perversely choose the base and evil, — in that, which
makes the living man leap up, as it were, in the strength of
sure conviction, which no arguments could bring, no dogmas of
Church or Council enforce, saying, as the Scripture words are
uttered, which answer to the Voice of Truth within, ' These

words are God's,— not the flesh, the outward matter, the mere letter, but the inward core and meaning of them,— for they are spirit, they are life.' As Dean MILMAN has observed, *Latin Christianity*, vi.p.633,—

What distinctness of conception, what precision of language, may be indispensable to true faith,—what part of the ancient dogmatic system may be allowed silently to fall into disuse, as at least superfluous, and as beyond the proper range of human thought and human language,—how far the sacred records may, without real peril to their truth, be subjected to closer investigation,—to what wider interpretation, especially of the Semitic portion, those records may submit, and wisely submit, in order to harmonise them with the irrefutable conclusions of science,—how far the Eastern veil of allegory which hangs over their truth may be lifted or torn away, to show their unshadowed essence,—how far the poetic vehicle, through which truth is conveyed, may be gently severed from the truth,—all this must be left to the future historian of our religion. As it is my own confident belief that the words of Christ, and His words alone, (the primal, indefeasible truths of Christianity,) shall not pass away, so I cannot presume to say that men may not attain to a clearer, at the same time more full and comprehensive and balanced, sense of those words, than has as yet been generally received in the Christian world. As all else is transient and mutable, these only eternal and universal, assuredly, whatever light may be thrown on the mental constitution of man, even on the constitution of nature, and the laws which govern the world, will be concentrated so as to give a more penetrating vision of those undying truths.

185. Thus, for instance, we may lead them to recognise the fact, that the third and sixth chapters of Exodus, which declare to us the Name of God,— ' I AM,' JEHOVAH, the Living God,— the Name of Him, 'in Whom we live, and move, and have our being,' upon Whom the whole universe depends,— whether written by Moses or by some other fellow-man, were yet written by one, who was specially inspired, first to conceive himself this transcendant, divine, thought, and then to express and tell it forth to others. To him first, in the secrets of his own inner being, was the revelation made of the nature and character of the Supreme, Self-existent, Being; and then he was moved by the self-same Spirit, and empowered with strength from above, to declare that Name, as an object of faith, to us. It matters not that the writer may have exhibited

the living Truth in the clothing of human imagery, and em-
bodied the divine lesson, which his own mind had received, and
which he felt himself commissioned to impart to his fellow-men,
in the story of the flaming bush and the audible voice. This
circumstance would not at all affect the nature of the Truth
itself, which remains still eternally true, whatever be the form
in which it is announced to us, — just as the truths, which our
Lord Himself teaches, are not the less true, because clothed in
the imagery of a parable, or of a narrative, (like that of Dives
and Lazarus, or of the good Samaritan,) which we do not suppose to be historically true. Such truths, however declared,
when once perceived by the spirit's eyes, are recognised at once
as truths, as eternal realities; and, being recognised, it would
be sinful not to believe and embrace them, as truths, which
God Himself, in His Providential dealings with man, has been
pleased to reveal to us, even through this imperfect agency.

186. But then, too, they must be taught to recognise the
voice of God's Spirit, in whatever way, by whatever ministry, He
vouchsafes to speak to the children of men; and to realise the
solid comfort of the thought, that, — not in the Bible only, but
also out of the Bible, — not to us Christians only, but to our
fellow-men of all climes and countries, ages and religions, — the
same Gracious Teacher is revealing, in different measures,
according to His own good pleasure, the hidden things of God.

As Prof. A. J. SCOTT observes, *Three Discourses &c., p.97,* —

What occurred in the case of Job, peculiar, probably, in degree, was surely not
in kind unexampled. The ancient Indian, who wrote that 'God is the gift of
charity, God is the offering, God is the fire of the altar, by God the sacrifice is
performed, and God is to be obtained by him, who makes God alone the object of
his work,' was one who had experienced somewhat of what Job had experienced,
or learned from one who had.

187. I quote, in proof of this, these noble words of CICERO,
preserved by LACTANTIUS, *Div. Inst.* vi.8 : —

Law, properly understood, is no other than right reason, agreeing with nature,
spread abroad among all men, ever consistent with itself, eternal, whose office is to

summon to duty by its commands, to deter from vice by its prohibitions, — which, however, to the good never commands or forbids in vain, never influences the wicked either by commanding or forbidding. In contradiction to this Law, nothing can be laid down, nor does it admit of partial or entire repeal. Nor can we be released from this Law either by vote of the Senate or decree of the people. Nor does it require any commentator or interpreter besides itself. Nor will there be one Law at Athens, and another at Rome, one now, and another hereafter: but one eternal, immutable, Law will both embrace all nations and at all times. And there will be one common Master, as it were, and Ruler of all, namely, God, the Great Originator, Expositor, Enactor, of this Law; which Law whoever will not obey, will be flying from himself, and, having treated with contempt his human nature, will in that very fact pay the greatest penalty, even if he shall have escaped other punishments, as they are commonly considered.

Well might the Christian philosopher observe that the heathen has here 'depicted that holy, heavenly, Law with a voice almost divine,' and that he regards such persons, 'speaking thus the truth without design,' as 'divining by some kind of Inspiration.'

188. And the same divine Teacher, we cannot doubt, revealed also to the Sikh Gooroos such great truths as these: (Cunningham's *History of the Sikhs*, p.355,356.)

The True Name is God, without fear, without enmity, the Being without Death, the Giver of Salvation.

Remember the primal Truth, Truth which was before the world began, Truth which is, and Truth, O Nanak, which will remain.

How can Truth be told? How can falsehood be unravelled?

O Nanak! by following the Will of God, as by Him ordained.

One Self-existent, Himself the Creator, O Nanak, One continueth, another never was, and never will be.

Thou art in each thing, and in all places; O God! Thou art the One Existent Being.

My mind dwells upon One, Him who gave the soul and the body.

Numerous Mahomets have there been, and multitudes of Brahmas, Vishnus, and Sivas,

Thousands of Peers and Prophets, and tens of thousands of Saints and Holy men;

But the Chief of Lords is the One Lord, the true Name of God.

O Nanak! of God, His qualities, without end, beyond reckoning, who can understand?

189. I quote also, in conclusion, the following words, which were written by one who had no Pentateuch or Bible to teach

him, but who surely learned such living truths as these by
the secret teaching of the Spirit of God. (*Journal of the
Asiatic Society of Bengal*, vi.p.484-487,750-756, quoted in
II. H. Wilson's *Works*.)

Whatever Rám willeth, that without the least difficulty shall be: why, therefore, do ye kill yourselves with grief, when grief can avail you nothing?

Whatsoever hath been made, God made. Whatsoever is to be made, God will make. Whatsoever is, God maketh. Then why do any of you afflict yourselves?

Thou, O God, art the Author of all things which have been made, and from Thee will originate all things which are to be made. Thou art the Maker and the Cause of all things made. There is none other but Thee.

He is my God, who maketh all things perfect. Meditate upon Him, in whose hands are life and death.

He is my God, who created heaven, earth, hell, and the intermediate space, who is the beginning and end of all creation, and who provideth for all.

I believe that God made man, and that He maketh every thing. He is my Friend.

Let faith in God characterise all your thoughts, words, and actions. He, who serveth God, places confidence in nothing else.

If the remembrance of God be in your hearts, ye will be able to accomplish things which are impracticable. But those who seek the paths of God are few!

O foolish one! God is not far from you: He is near you. You are ignorant; but He knoweth every thing, and is careful in bestowing.

Care can avail nothing; it devoureth life: for those things shall happen, which God shall direct.

Remember God, for He endued your body with life: remember that Beloved One, who placed you in the womb, reared and nourished you.

Preserve God in your hearts, and put faith in your minds, so that by God's power your expectations may be realised.

In order that He may diffuse happiness, God becometh subservient to all; and, although the knowledge of this is in the hearts of the foolish, yet will they not praise His Name.

O God, Thou art, as it were, exceeding riches; Thy regulations are without compare; Thou art the chief of every world, yet remainest invisible.

Take such food and raiment, as it may please God to provide you with: you require naught besides.

He, that partaketh of but one grain of the Love of God, shall be released from the sinfulness of all his doubts and actions.

I take for my spiritual food the water and the leaf of Rám. In the world I care not; but God's Love is unfathomable.

What hope can those have elsewhere, even if they wandered over the whole earth, who abandon God?

It will be impossible for you to profit anything, if you are not with God, even if you were to wander from country to country.

Have no desires, but accept what circumstances may bring before you; because, whatever God pleaseth to direct, can never be wrong.

All things are exceeding sweet to those who love God; they would never style them bitter, even if filled with poison; on the contrary, they would accept them as if they were ambrosia.

Adversity is good, if on account of God; but it is useless to pain the body. Without God, the comforts of wealth are unprofitable.

Whatever is to be, will be; therefore long not for grief, nor for joy; because by seeking the one, you may find the other. Forget not to praise God.

Do unto me, O God, as Thou thinkest best: I am obedient to Thee. My disciples! behold no other God; go nowhere but to Him.

Condemn none of those things, which the Creator hath made. Those are His holy servants, who are satisfied with them.

We are not creators: the Creator is a distinct Being: He can make whatever He desireth, but we can make nothing.

God is my clothing and my dwelling: He is my ruler, my body, and my soul.

God ever fostereth His creatures, even as a mother serves her offspring, and keepeth it from harm.

O God, Thou who art the Truth, grant me contentment, love, devotion, and faith. Thy servant prayeth for true patience, and that he may be devoted to Thee.

He, that formed the mind, made it as it were a temple for Himself to dwell in; for God liveth in the mind, and none other but God.

O my friend, recognise that Being, with whom thou art so intimately connected; think not that God is distant, but believe that, like thy own shadow, He is ever near thee.

Receive that which is perfect into your hearts, to the exclusion of all besides; abandon all things for the love of God, for this Didô declares is the true devotion.

All have it in their power to take away their own lives, but they cannot release their souls from punishment; for God alone is able to pardon the soul, though few deserve His Mercy.

If you call upon God, you will be able to subdue your imperfections, and the evil inclinations of your mind will depart from you; but they will return to you again, when you cease to call upon Him.

INDEX OF TEXTS.

END OF PART I.

www.ingramcontent.com/pod-product-compliance
Lightning Source LLC
Chambersburg PA
CBHW030837270326
41928CB00007B/1088